Suleika Jaouad

Biography

A Life Interrupted

CONTENT

Part One

Chapter 1: The Itch

Chapter 2: Eggshells

Chapter 3: Bifurcation

Chapter 4: Bubble Girl

Chapter 5: The Hundred-Day Project

Chapter 6: On Opposite Ends of a Telescope

Chapter 7: Hope Lodge

Chapter 8: Chronology of Freedom

Chapter 9: The Last Good Night

Part Two

Chapter 10: The In-Between Place

Chapter 11: Reentry

Chapter 12: Written on the Skin

Chapter 13: The Value of Pain

Chapter 14: Homegoing

Part One

Chapter 1: The Itch

Initially, there was an itch. It's a real, physical itch, not a quarter-life crisis or a metaphorical desire to see the world. During my final year of college, I had a terrible, itchy, and sleep-depriving itch that started on the tips of my feet and progressed up my calves and thighs. I made an effort not to scratch, but the itching persisted and spread like a thousand unseen mosquito bites across my skin. Unaware of my actions, my hand started to wander down my legs, my fingernails searching my pants for solace before digging beneath the hem and digging straight into flesh. While working part-time in the college film lab, I itched. Under my library carrel's large oak desk, I itched. Dancing with friends on the beer-stained floors of taprooms in basements made me itchy. As I slept, I itched. As soon as my legs were pummeled with rose thistles, they were covered in a scree of bleeding nicks, thick scabs, and new scars. Bloody signs of an internal conflict that is intensifying.

Before sending me off with bitter teas and odorous vitamins, a Chinese herbalist told me, "It might be a parasite you picked up while studying abroad." It might be eczema, according to a nurse at the college health center, who suggested a cream. A medical practitioner offered me samples of an anti-anxiety drug after speculating that it was stress-related. I tried not to worry too much about it, though, because nobody seemed to know for sure. I hoped things would work itself out.

Before anyone could see my limbs, I would open my dorm room door, look around the hallway, and run in my towel to the shared restroom every morning. I used a moist cloth to cleanse my skin while seeing the red striations as they moved down the shower drain. I covered myself with witch hazel tonic-based pharmacy concoctions and covered my nose while consuming the bitter tea mixtures. When it became too hot to wear jeans every day, I bought a pair of opaque black tights. To cover up the rusty streaks, I bought black sheets. Additionally, I had sex while the lights were off.

The naps followed the itching. The two-hour, four-hour, and six-hour naps. Sleep seemed to have no effect on my physique. I started nodding off during supper, deadlines, job interviews, and symphony practices, only to wake up feeling even more exhausted. One day, while we were walking to class, I told my pals, "I've never felt so tired in my life." They sympathized, "Me too, me too." Everyone was worn out. Due to a mixture of working long hours at the library to complete our senior theses and attending wild parties that continued until dawn, we had seen more sunrises in the past semester than we had in our whole lives. I resided on the top floor of a Gothic-style dorm with turrets and grimacing gargoyles in the center of the Princeton campus. My pals would gather in my room for a final nightcap at the conclusion of another late night. My room had large cathedral windows, and we enjoyed sitting on the sills with our legs hanging over the side to watch the first amber rays streak the stone-paved courtyard and intoxicated revelers stumble home. With graduation approaching, we were resolved to make the most of these last few weeks together before we all parted ways, even if it meant straining our bodies to the breaking point.

But I was concerned that my level of weariness was different.

When everyone had left and I was alone in my bed, I felt like there was a feast going on beneath my skin, something nibbling at my sanity as it wound its way through my arteries. I convinced myself that the parasite's appetite was expanding as my energy level dropped and the itching got worse. However, I secretly questioned whether a parasite ever existed. I started to question whether I was the true issue.

I felt adrift and on the verge of sinking in the months that followed, clinging to anything that could keep me afloat. I was able for a while. After graduating, I moved to New York City with my friends. On Craigslist, I came upon a listing for a spare bedroom in a spacious, floor-through loft above a Canal Street art supply company. In the summer of 2010, the city was depleted of oxygen due to a heat wave. The smell of rotting trash hit me square in the face as I stepped out of the subway. On the walkways, commuters and crowds of visitors looking to buy fake designer bags bumped into one another. Sweat had made my white tank top transparent by the time I dragged my bag to the front door of the third-floor walk-up apartment. There were nine new roommates, so I introduced myself. Three performers, two models, a chef, a jewelry designer, a doctoral student, and a financial analyst were all in their twenties and trying to be something or other. We each had our own windowless dungeon, divided by paper-thin drywall, which was constructed by a slumlord to maximize his profits, for eight hundred dollars a month.

When I arrived on my first day of my summer work at the Center for Constitutional Rights, I was amazed to see some of the nation's most courageous civil rights attorneys. Although the internship was unpaid and living in New York City felt like going around with a huge hole in my wallet, the work felt significant. I spent the two thousand bucks I had saved during the academic year in a flash. I was barely making ends meet, even with my evening gigs at the restaurant and babysitting.

I was terrified to think about my future, vast but empty. And it delighted me, too, when I let myself fantasize. The potential of who I could be and where I could end up felt limitless, like a spool of ribbon unfolding far beyond what my imagination could perceive. My dad is from North Africa, where I briefly lived as a child, and I had dreamed of working there as a foreign journalist. I also considered going to law school, which seemed like a wiser course of action. To be honest, I needed money. Due to my full scholarship, I had only been allowed to attend an Ivy League university. However, unlike many of my classmates, I did not have the same safety nets in the real world, such as trust money, family ties, or six-figure Wall Street positions.

It was simpler to worry about the unknown than to face yet another, more disturbing change. I drank caffeinated energy drinks during my final semester to fight off the exhaustion. A boy I had dated briefly offered me some of his Adderall to get through exams when they stopped working. However, that eventually proved insufficient as well. There were usually individuals hanging about who supplied a line here and there for free, and cocaine was a party mainstay in my group of friends. No one objected when I began to participate. It had turned out that my roommates in the loft on Canal Street were also hard-partying people. In order to prevent my growing fatigue, I started taking uppers in the same manner that some people add an additional shot of espresso to their coffee. I wrote in my journal: Stay afloat.

By the end of summer, I was having trouble identifying myself. My alarm clock's muffled tone sliced through my restless slumber like a dull knife. I would stutter out of bed every morning and stand in front of the floor-length mirror, assessing the damage. My legs were covered in fresh spots with scratches and lines of drying blood. I was too exhausted to brush the drab, tangled locks of hair that hung to my waist. Under large bloodshot eyes, shadowy crescents deepened into dark moons. I started arriving at my internship later and later because I was too exhausted to face the sun, and eventually I stopped going altogether.

I didn't like who I was becoming: someone who threw herself into every day, constantly moving but without direction; someone who, like a private investigator, recreated blackouts night after night; someone who consistently broke promises; someone too ashamed to answer her parents' phone calls. I looked disgustedly at my mirror and thought, "This isn't me." I had to get my act together. I had to get a legitimate job that paid. I needed to go away from my roommates on Canal Street and my college pals. It was imperative that I leave New York City as quickly as possible.

A few days after ending the internship, I got up early one August morning, brought my laptop outside to the fire escape, and began looking for work. The summer had been dry and sunny, and the heat had baked my skin tan, leaving my legs covered in tiny white spots that resembled braille where the scratching had left scars. On the spur of the moment, I applied for a paralegal employment at an American law firm in Paris. I worked on my cover letter all day. In an attempt to gain an advantage, I made careful to note that my first language was French and that I could also speak Arabic. Being a paralegal sounded like the kind of thing a sensible person might pursue, but it wasn't my ideal career—I didn't even really know what it entailed. For the most part, I believed that a change of environment would help me stop acting recklessly. Paris was my getaway plan, not a destination on my bucket list.

Chapter 2: Eggshells

Since I was seventeen, I haven't been single for more than a month or two. Although I didn't think it was healthy and I wasn't proud of it, that was the way things had been. I was in a committed relationship with a bright British-Chinese comparative literature major for the majority of my time in college. As the semesters went by, I became restless and wished I had more experience before meeting him. He was my first true boyfriend, and he brought me to upscale meals in the city and on vacation to Waikiki Beach. That relationship ended when I had a passionate affair with a young Ethiopian filmmaker the summer before my senior year. After that, I met a Bostonian who had recently been arrested for lowering a thirty-foot Palestinian flag down the side of one of the pyramids while conducting research in Cairo during winter break. He had a penchant for large-scale stunts and activism. He called his folks a week later as we were sipping bootleg whiskey at a bar with a view of the Red Sea. Before I could object, he handed me the phone and said, "Meet the girl I'm gonna marry." Shortly afterward, I ended our relationship. I began dating the ambitious Mexican-Texan screenwriter around graduation. He tended tables at a hip downtown hotel while I interned in New York, and we dated for two awful months. He was intoxicated most of the time, and when he was, he became cruel.

These partnerships were everything but casual. I was really engrossed in them at the time, engrossed in the thought of living with them. But even at the worst of times, I could see a faintly lit exit sign in the distance—and, in all honesty, I was always about to bolt for it. I loved the concept of being in love. To put it another way, I was too young to be preoccupied with broken promises because I was too impetuous and careless with other people's feelings, too preoccupied with myself, and too preoccupied with finding out what would happen next.

It was different with Will. I had never dated a man like him before. He was a strange mix of academic, class clown, and jock, and he could dunk a basketball as easily as he could recite lyrics from poetry by W. B. Yeats. I was struck by how considerate he was and how determined he was to put everyone in the room at ease. He was five years older than me, but he had a calm, modest wisdom and a carefree personality that made him appear both much younger and much older than his actual age. The exit sign vanished from sight the instant Will arrived back at the door of my Paris apartment, this time carrying a large duffel bag full of everything he owned. I gave it my all.

I emptied the bookshelves to make way for Will's possessions, and he unpacked and folded his clothes into tidy little stacks. He rummaged through his duffle bag, took out a portable speaker, and requested permission to play some music. Hip-hop from the 1990s, featuring Warren G, was playing nonstop in the apartment. As he danced around the hardwood floor and rapped along to the words, I couldn't help but laugh. Almost tipping over a cooking pan, he grabbed my hand and twirled me around the kitchen.

I used a dish towel to slap him away and replied, "You're distracting me."

I wanted to show Will how good I was at cooking, so I began preparing shepherd's pie for lunch. I cooked beef, mashed potatoes, sautéed shallots, and sliced carrots with intense focus. I had contacted my mom earlier that morning to get the recipe because it was the first homemade food I had ever tried, aside from scrambled eggs, the occasional bowl of pasta, and my favorite dinner of Nutella toast. It was hot in the kitchen, which was about the size of a small utility closet and had neither windows nor a fan for air. When I placed all the ingredients in a casserole dish, added some cheese on top, and baked the entire mess, my forehead beaded again after I wiped it with the dish towel. The smell of butter and fresh herbs soon filled the flat, giving it a homey scent for the first time.

Will was on the steamer trunk in the other room, arranging the table. I opened the windows to let some fresh air in and joined him. A few slow flakes drifted inside the flat from the snow that had begun to fall outside. At the window, Will joined me and drew me to him by wrapping his arms around my waist. He put his face in my hair and murmured, "I'll start looking for work tomorrow." "At the very least, until I can say in French, 'I'll have three baguettes and an Orangina, please,' I should find a language school where I can take lessons."

Will's torso muscles felt warm and tense against my shoulder blades. I tried to recall the last time I had felt this joyful as I closed my eyes and melted into him. couldn't. Will retreated and said, "Stay right there." He took his camera from the bookshelf and took a picture of me standing in front of the window, silhouetted against the winter sky. I was startled by my appearance when he showed me the picture. My skin appeared so pale that it was almost transparent. I had robin's-egg blue eyelashes, as though every vein had risen to the surface. My lips appeared to be devoid of vitality.

Will's 27th birthday came two weeks later. I took a few days off work to celebrate his birthday and recent move, and I sent him an envelope with two train tickets to Amsterdam as a surprise. Our breath caught in the crisp morning air as we exited the station in January 2011. Our goal was to walk around the city. The schedule includes a boat tour of the canals, a stop at the market to enjoy pickled herring, and a visit to the Anne Frank House. However, we didn't get too far. I stopped every block or so, my temples pounding like tuning forks, a deep cough racking my body, leaving me lightheaded and dizzy.

We ended up spending the majority of the weekend at our shady, two-star hotel in the red-light area because I felt so shabby. Burn marks were visible on the hotel's bedding, a dirty window viewed a canal, and the sound of a malfunctioning radiator reverberated through the gloomy hallways. However, the thing about being in love is that it feels like an adventure and you can be anywhere. I had really turned to him when we first arrived and exclaimed, "This is my favorite hotel ever!" with excitement.

Despite my poor health, I was determined to make our first trip together one to remember. This is how I ended up in a basement coffee shop on the afternoon of Will's birthday, purchasing a tin of psychedelic mushrooms from a dreadlocked, gangly white lad. I told Will, who had never tried them before and appeared nervous, to "come on, don't be a square." "All right," he finally said. This is humanity's final year, if the Mayans were correct. Let's do it correctly. When the server wasn't looking, I scattered a handful of the mushrooms over a hearty stew of spiced lentils at an Ethiopian restaurant where we were having supper after walking a few blocks. "You know that you're a nut?" Will picked up the laced lentils with a piece of injera flat a dubious manner while laughing and shaking his head at me.

After supper, we made our way back to the hotel while the fog lingered low over the city. We trudged across frozen bridges and through slushy streets, dodging bicycles who flew by and rang their bells. We saw figures glowing behind curtained windows as we strolled through the red-light district. Before exploding into a rainbow, a traffic light changed from orange to red to green. From where we were standing, I could see our hotel's neon sign flickering like an ember. In an attempt to get to our room before the medications took full effect, we accelerated our speed. By the time we entered, my skin's pores had transformed into tiny flame-emitting torches. In an effort to chill down, I ripped off all of my clothing and lay down on the mattress. As this was going on, Will started constructing a tent over the bed out of pillows and linens. I patted the empty spot beside me and said, "Come in, it's really gezellig." Our new favorite term was gezellig, an untranslatable Dutch expression that roughly translates to "cozy." Will lay down next to me after sliding beneath the cover of sheets.

With a palm on my forehead, he said, "Jesus, you're burning up."

At the time, I assumed it simply meant that the medications were effective. However, my fever increased steadily over the course of the following several hours, until I felt as though my body may explode. I began to tremble. I recall feeling vulnerable for the first time in my life as rivulets of sweat gathered in the clefts of my collarbones. "I feel like I'm extremely cautious," I repeatedly told him. "Are you okay with us staying here forever?"

Will became worried and recommended that we visit the emergency department. "I'll look after you," he said.

I showed him my bicep and replied, "Non merci, I am tough."

"We'll be back before you know it if we take a taxi there."

I resisted until he gave up, nodding my head no. Being one of those foolish tourists who went to Amsterdam, took a lot of mushrooms, and ended up in the hospital was not something I wanted to happen.

We took a train back to Paris the following afternoon. That sense of vulnerability persisted even after the fever and hallucinations subsided. I felt weaker and less energetic every day. It seemed like someone was erasing my innermost thoughts. My insides were muting into a ghostly palimpsest, but the outline of my former personality was still there.

Chapter 3: Bifurcation

I had been back home for a week. I have a vague memory of how I spent the time. I skyped with Will, went to a bunch of doctor's visits, and slept a lot. Along with my folks, I grudgingly dragged myself out for walks around the neighborhood. The uneasy silence that had descended upon the home, the worry that pervaded the atmosphere, and the growing fear and frustration I had while I awaited clarity, however, are the things I remember most.

I wrote in my journal that I destroyed Easter today. Anne prepared a fantastic dinner for Dad and me over the course of six hours. I didn't eat anything, and all I could do was look at them both with a sad expression. I am terrified of the bone marrow biopsy I have scheduled for this Wednesday.

When the doctor recommended the biopsy, he used the word "precautionary." Lying facedown on an examination table with my jeans around my ankles was a painful, humiliating process. As he explained that the pelvic bone, which is rich in marrow, was the ideal site for the biopsy, the doctor used betadine to clean my lower back. The needle was inserted deeper and deeper until it hit bone while he administered anesthetic to my lower back. The doctor cautioned that it would hurt even if my skin's outer layers were numb. He aspirated the marrow cells with rapid, nauseating swallows while inserting a thin syringe into the bone, and I clinched my teeth. Then a much larger needle arrived, ten inches of shiny stainless steel with a plastic handle on top, which he would use to cut into the marrow more deeply. The doctor grunted as he drilled into my pelvic bone and placed one shoe on the examination table, saying, "My bones were young and strong." I tasted blood as I bit the inside of my cheek as he cut off a tiny, solid piece of marrow. My back ached as I sat there bewildered after the procedure, with a large bandage covering the biopsy site. Although he didn't anticipate discovering anything unusual, the doctor wanted to take every precaution because of my deteriorating health.

Chapter 4: Bubble Girl

IT WAS The sky was a clear, bright blue on this ideal spring morning on Manhattan's Upper East Side. After parking the minivan, we made our way past the line of uniformed doormen on Fifth Avenue and walked the 10 streets to Mount Sinai Hospital. I saw the clouds, like tissue paper, floating thinly overhead. I saw Central Park, which was a riot of color, with the delicate yellow tulips rising from the ground, the fuchsia spray of azalea bushes, and the lush greens of fresh leaves emerging from trees. I tried to recollect the sensation of the sun on my hair and the way the spring air brushed across the back of my neck when I opened my eyes wider.

My parents took a moment to give me a silver necklace with a turquoise charm when we arrived at the stairs leading to the main door of the hospital. My mother continued, "I'll give you another charm for every new milestone you reach in your treatment," with a smile on her lips and a grief in her eyes that I had never seen before. Will also gave me a purple Moleskine notebook as a gift. Inside, under "In case of loss please return to:," he had written "$1,000,000 reward if returned to the owner" and my childhood nickname, "Susu." I took a final breath of fresh air as we opened the glass doors and entered, holding it in my lungs for as long as I could because I knew it would be a while before I was permitted to go outside again.

I was led upstairs to the oncology unit, where I was placed in a dull room with two hospital beds and stark white walls. I picked the one nearest the window because both were unoccupied. I changed into a backless hospital gown after hanging my favorite summer dress in the wardrobe like a sportsman retiring a jersey. An electronic bracelet was fastened to my right wrist as a preventative measure against patients who attempted to leave the hospital when high on painkillers or dazed by dementia. I can't even remember how many paperwork I signed, one of which named my mother as my healthcare proxy. I completed an advance directive as well. After that, I was hauled off to surgery, where a central line was created in my chest using a catheter so that I could receive intravenous fluids and chemotherapy.

I awoke in the surgical recovery room and stared down at my chest, which was covered in blood. A plastic tube with three dangling lumens, resembling the tentacles of some repulsive sea creature, protruded from an incision beneath my collarbone. I was astonished to see my changed body. I threw up while leaning over the gurney's railings. Except for the mouth sores, my condition had been virtually undetectable until now. On some way, I was beginning to see that my previous existence had been destroyed—the person I had been had been buried. Never would I be the same. My name had even been altered, albeit unintentionally. I saw the sign outside my hospital room read S. Jaquad—with a q where the o should be—as I was taken back to the oncology ward. I was entering a new territory. And I felt less like Suleika with each stride.

Two nurses came into my room with IV bags filled with chemotherapy and antiemetic drugs that would be injected into my veins for the next seven days. Younique was the name the younger nurse gave. Her jet-black, hot-combed hair was put up into a manageable knot, and she appeared to be around my age. I gave her the doubtful look of someone who is going to let a complete stranger poison her. Younique pointed to the smaller of the two bags and said, "Be on the lookout for that little guy." It was the hue of fruit punch and contained one of the chemotherapy medications. Because of its often unpleasant adverse effects, some people refer to it as the Red Devil. Just press the call button if you need anything.

Sitting on folding chairs, Will and my parents watched me till the sun outside the window turned from a bright white to a shady orange. I kept the silences filled with meaningless banter and stupid jokes. Along with my favorite stuffed animal and slippers from home, I also took a stack of novels that I planned to read through while I was in the hospital. As I picked up Tolstoy's War and Peace and turned the pages, I exclaimed, "I feel like I just moved into a dorm room on the first day of college." "I'll have time to read more." While I'm here, I might even be able to write something.

I did want to charge forward, to try to do something, and I meant it. Since receiving my diagnosis, I'd been running on a strange high, with dread and adrenaline pumping through my veins and a frantic sense of optimism. I was positive that nothing would shatter me, not even the terrible illness ripping through my blood and bone marrow, the spartan melancholy of this hospital room, or the horrifying side effects of the treatment that was yet to come. This event would, if anything, strengthen me. Who could have known? I might even become one of those people who had cancer and went on to run ultramarathons or start a research foundation. However, my main goal was to reassure my parents and Will that I would be alright and to lessen the anxiety that was weighing on their faces. As I rambled on, they gave me a feeble smile and whispered encouraging things.

The sky eventually grew darker. I told Will and my parents, who were staying at our family friend's apartment a few blocks away, to go home and rest. They didn't move, but they appeared worn out. They only got up to go when I pushed them to. My mother hung around the door and questioned, "Are you sure you'll be all right on your own?" I pleasantly waved them away and added, "I'm great."

The brave mask I had been wearing all day only started to fold and collapse after they left.

More than any other area in the planet, oncology wards are devoid of music. Continuous beeping takes the place of a flowing tune. Throughout the day, the hallways are filled with a never-ending medical call-and-response cycle: nurses shouting at each other, patients phoning—sometimes yelling—for morphine, nurses rushing to locate doctors, and visitors desperately looking for nurses. Despite their annoyance, those sounds serve as a pleasant diversion and a reminder that the hospital "machine" is functioning well. What is most terrifying are the quiet hours after dark, the empty sounds of silent anguish.

Before going to bed, Younique had given me an Ambien. In a matter of minutes, I was driven into a deep sleep, where I dreamed of all the patients who had previously slept on the same hospital pillow as me, their pale faces glimmering in my mind. I woke up at 2:00 a.m., groggy and confused, roused from my nightmares by the sound of whimpering. I initially believed I might be having hallucinations, but after turning on the light, I saw that I had a roommate—a woman in her seventies who had come in the middle of the night. She panted quickly and sharply through broken lips, her eyes clenched shut and her mouth contorted in pain. She groaned as she tossed and turned in a daze from the drugs. I got a preview of what was to come when I saw this stranger, immersed in her suffering. Not wanting to see any more, I closed the gauzy green curtain between our beds and flicked off the light. In an attempt to regain the courage and hope I had felt earlier in the day, I closed my eyes. Rather, I discovered just fear.

I took up the phone and called Will as quietly as possible. He asked in a sleep-felt voice, "What's wrong?" I opened my mouth to speak, but nothing came out. He said, "I'll be right there; I'm getting into a cab."

His lanky figure filled the doorway thirty minutes later. His big legs squirmed over the edge of my hospital bed as he tiptoed past my new roommate to my side of the room and wriggled in next to me. What occurs if an NBA player develops cancer? Do they need to order extra-long, specially constructed hospital beds? I muttered. "Nice query," Will answered. "Just be happy that you are the patient." We lay forehead to forehead when I scooted to the top of the mattress. Feeling like a bundle of clean laundry, I slackened into Will's arms and breathed in his warm, soapy aroma.

Chapter 5: The Hundred-Day Project

The therapist my parents made me start seeing said, "YOU NEED TO find a hobby, something you can do that's within your physical limitations." Her comments were an epiphany to me at the time, but they seem clear now. In the context of my previous life, the wedding, the creative writing class, the GRE, the graduate school applications, and the outing to the mall with Molly would have all made sense. I had to find something I could do while in bed at the hospital or at home. In addition to acknowledging my limitations—the fatigue and nausea, the mental haze, and the frequent hospital stays—I also needed to find a way to turn my suffering into something constructive.

The therapist said, "I've heard baking can be pretty calming." There, she lost me. Such recommendations were frequently made to me. Volunteers from the hospital provided a range of activities to break up the day, including dream catchers, vision boards, and knitting and beading. I received board games, "adult" coloring books, and jigsaw puzzles from friends. However, none of these pursuits felt particularly me. I wanted to state that I'm not in preschool or retired, but I'm unwell.

Ultimately, however, I consented to test what we termed the Hundred-Day Project. I'm not sure who thought of it first, but the plan was for Will, my family, and I to set aside a little period of time each day for the following 100 days to concentrate on a creative project. Originally intended to be a means of structuring our lives around a single, modest act of creativity, the project evolved into much more.

Will chose to send me daily video broadcasts from the outside regarding everything from the weather to the quality of the pizza in the hospital cafeteria as part of his Hundred-Day Project. In one, he stated, "I'm reporting live from Central Park today." "Let me introduce you to my favorite vendor of hot dogs. Tell Suleika "what up," Rafiki. Every time I felt lonely, I viewed the videos again and again. I occasionally feared that we were getting too far apart, but the films gave me a sense of connection to him and the world beyond my window.

My mother, on the other hand, made the decision to paint a single little ceramic tile by hand every morning. She completed the job by assembling the tiles into a large, multicolored mosaic, which she then put on my bedroom wall. She referred to it as "Suleika's Shield" and told me it had protecting abilities. She attempted to conceal her suffering in the artwork, but I questioned whether the pictures, which primarily featured distressed birds—falling, upside down, with their beaks open in desperation—reflected her actual mental state. One tile mentioned is "le coeur qui saigne," or "the heart that bleeds."

On Christmas morning, my father gave me a small book that contained 101 of his childhood recollections, which he had printed and bound for his project. I got a genuine look into his past for the first time. He talked of the yearly springtime trips his family took to the Matmata caves in Tunisia to visit the shrine of the patron saint Sidi Gnaw. He described how my great-great-grandmother Oumi 'Ouisha, the local healer, would whisper incantations into her patients' ears while sending my father to retrieve the herbs and desert plants she kept beneath her bed. He described how, as a little child, he was shocked to see colonial expats lounging in Speedos and bikinis on the "French beach" across town. When our women had a yearly sea bath during Awossu, they waded knee-deep into the water while completely dressed. We referred to them as "floating tents."

Long after I read one entry, it continued to torment me. It told of Gmar, the younger sister of my father, the one "with the beautiful face." Her name, which translates to "moon" in Arabic, was unfamiliar to me; in fact, I had never heard anyone in my extended family mention it. As I continued reading, I realized why. Gmar had been bedridden for the majority of her brief life due to an unexplained illness, until one hot summer morning when, in my father's words, "she expired." Even at the age of four, he could still hear his mother's cries reverberating around the home when Gmar passed away. He was afraid of bringing up unpleasant memories, so he never ventured to ask her what had happened to Gmar. As far as I knew, my father's side of the family had no history of cancer, but after reading the narrative, I couldn't help but wonder if Gmar and I had the same diagnosis. Strangely enough, knowing that I wasn't alone was consoling.

Regarding my Hundred-Day Project, I made the decision to go back to journaling, which I had always relied on during trying times. I made a commitment to myself to attempt to write something every day, even if it was just a sentence, regardless of how ill or worn out I felt.

Words did not fail me that day, the next, or after—instead, they flowed out of me hesitantly at first, then exuberantly, my mind waking as if from a long sleep, thoughts pouring out quicker than my pen could keep up. People frequently react to the news of tragedy by saying, "Words fail." This was not like any writing I had ever done before. It has nothing to do with the future. Every sentence was rooted in the present. I had always thought of myself as the type of writer who would assist others in sharing their tales, but I was finding that I was more and more drawn to the first person. I was looking inwards because I was sick.

You are continuously prompted to examine your body, report on yourself, and describe your findings as a patient. For example, how are you feeling? On a scale of 1 to 10, how much pain do you feel? Have you developed any new symptoms? Are you prepared to return home? I now saw why so many artists and writers turned to memoir writing when they were really ill. It gave you a sense of empowerment and the ability to change your situation according to your own terms and preferences. Jeanette Winterson observed, "That is what literature offers—a language powerful enough to say how it is." It's not a place to hide. It is a site of discovery.

Naturally, there were days when I was too exhausted to write much, but journaling helped me rediscover my love of words and was the catalyst for me to start reading regularly again. I looked through the hardbound copy of The Diary of Frida Kahlo that my mother had given me. I was touched to hear that Kahlo had been a premedical student in Mexico City, not much younger than I was when leukemia hit. Her bus once struck a streetcar on the way home from school. She sustained fractures to her elbow, pelvis, leg, ribs, spine, and clavicle. Her left shoulder was dislocated, and her right foot was crushed. The iron railing of the streetcar punctured her, entering through her left hip and leaving through her pelvic floor. She spent months in bed as a result of the injuries.

Kahlo's dream was to become a doctor before the accident. She later had to scrap those ambitions, but spending so much time at home recovering forced her to find a new passion. "I didn't consider painting until 1926, while I was recovering from a car accident," she remarked. I made the decision to do anything since I was quite bored while in bed wearing a plaster cast. I started painting after [stealing] some oil paints from my father and getting a customized easel from my mother because I was unable to sit [up].

Kahlo turned her captivity into a space brimming with symbolism and significance. She started painting the self-portraits that would establish her as one of the most well-known artists of all time, using a little lap easel and a mirror suspended in the canopy of her bed so she could see her reflection. However, Kahlo's initial canvas, which she repeatedly revisited, was the body itself—the plaster corset she wore to support her broken back. She owned dozens of corsets throughout her life, which would shape her life and work. They were both torment and beauty, inspiration and incarceration. She embellished each one, covering the plaster with bits of cloth and pictures of streetcars, tigers, monkeys, and birds with vivid plumage. She occasionally painted her tears and scars. She remarked, "I paint myself because I am so alone so often." "I am the subject I know best, and I am also my own muse." the topic I'd like to learn more about.

After her death, Kahlo's paintings preserved her operations and recuperations, her infatuations and heartbreaks, and she became almost legendary as a patroness of misfits and victims. Was it ever possible for someone in good health to create these masterpieces? I pondered. Could they have been made by someone who hadn't had to face the human body's awful fragility? I wasn't certain.

Naturally, I wasn't Frida Kahlo, so it was still hard for me to think of a creative way to deal with my own bad luck. However, something within me had been sparked by her story. I started looking into the lengthy history of bedridden authors and artists who turned their pain into inspiration: In order to complete his design for the Chapel of the Rosary in Venice while recuperating from intestinal cancer, Henri Matisse attached a paintbrush to a long pole so he could work from bed and acted as though the ceiling of his room was the chapel. Due to chronic asthma and sadness that had afflicted him since infancy, Marcel Proust had to live in a prone position. He wrote his seven-volume epic, In Search of Lost Time, from a tiny brass bed in his bedroom that was coated with cork to keep out outside noise. In a letter to a friend, Roald Dahl expressed his belief that his chronic pain had served as the catalyst for his writing career: "I doubt I would have written a line, or would have had the ability to write a line, unless some minor tragedy had sort of twisted my mind out of the normal rut." The physical limitations and other ways in which life was foreclosed seemed to boost creativity and productivity in each of these situations. "Feet, what do I need you for when I have wings to fly?" Kahlo wrote.

I made the decision to reframe my survival as an artistic endeavor. I would discover different ways to communicate if talking was too painful due to the chemo sores in my mouth. As long as I remained in bed, my imagination would serve as the means by which I was able to leave my room. I would reassess my priorities and make the most of my time if my body had become so exhausted that I only had three functional hours every day.

In light of this, I rearranged my bedroom so that everything I needed was close at hand: a bookshelf stocked with my favorite novels and poetry books; a wooden board that I used as a desk on my knees; and a little night table covered in pencils, notes, and paper. I blogged every day that I ended up back in the hospital, as well as when I was at home. I wrote until the agony, resentment, and jealousy drained away—until I was unable to hear the incessant sirens, the hiss of respirators, and the beep of monitors. For the time being, I knew that I was beginning to discover my strength, but I had no way of knowing where the Hundred-Day Project would lead me.

Chapter 6: On Opposite Ends of a Telescope

My eyes were wide as I lay in my hospital bed beneath a halo of hanging IV bags on my first night in the bone marrow transplant unit. I was alive with fear. I could feel its hot breath chuffing across my skin and smell its damp fur throughout the room. After folding the covers, I got out of bed and crossed the dense tangle of cables and tubes that linked me to a number of equipment. I lowered myself on my hands and knees, just like my late friend Yehya had done, pressing my forehead against the cool linoleum so as not to hit my skull. I had grown up with a jumble of customs and beliefs because my mother had been raised Catholic and my father had been raised Muslim. We observed Easter and attended Mass when we were with our Swiss relatives; we fasted during Ramadan and killed a lamb on Eid when we were with our Tunisian relatives; and we continued to live a largely secular life in the United States, except for Christmas. Despite my lifelong fascination with religion, I had never been a true practitioner. I wasn't sure how or to whom to pray, but I was certain that I needed all the support I could receive.

What specifically was I requesting? In this same hospital room, how many other desperate people had attempted to negotiate with a higher power? My thin legs were shaking under my weight, and I was starting to feel lightheaded. I got up, picked up a glow-in-the-dark pen that a buddy had given me, and headed toward the wall. I had nothing poetic or eloquent to say. Let me live, I scribbled in small letters, part prayer, part plea, just one plain, animal wish.

My new surroundings added to the intensity of the occasion. I had made the decision to move from Mount Sinai to Memorial Sloan Kettering Cancer Center, which was regarded as the best transplant unit in the city, if not the nation, after doing some research on the best transplant units. I still worried about the choice. Aside from the glitzy pamphlets and quick meet-and-greets, shopping for bone marrow transplant units had been similar to browsing colleges; only time would tell if I had made the proper decision. I had the impression that I had stepped into an extraterrestrial spaceship in Sloan Kettering's transplant facility, complete with futuristic equipment, beeping monitors, and strange faces wearing masks and surgical gowns. I missed the inside jokes, quirky intelligence, and burning compassion of my medical staff, including Dr. Holland. My doctors and nurses had become like extended family over the past year. When we said our goodbyes, Younique had promised me that she would return to see me when she was feeling better.

Farewells have filled the past week. Saratoga was where I spent my last few days before going into the transplant unit. As I prepared my red luggage for the eight-week hospital stay, I threw in Sleepy, the stuffed animal I had loved as a child, at the last minute. I woke up at five o'clock and explored the house because I couldn't sleep the night before I left. I said farewell to the pink walls, bookshelves, and old favorite posters in my childhood bedroom as I took one last glance. I also bid my bass farewell by rubbing a palm across its wooden nape. I bid farewell to my mother's garden's frozen flower beds and the dining room table, where we had eaten innumerable family meals over the years. After loading our stuff into the car, Will and my parents came down for breakfast. As the minivan drove away from the house, I was filled with a deep sense of loss and wondered if I would ever be able to go back. In the present tense, mourning for the dying person starts with a sequence of private, proactive farewells that happen long before the body's final breath.

I was surrounded by folks in the transplant unit who were more interested in what I had than in who I was. Mask-wearing nurses and doctors stood over my hospital bed, looking down at me and talking about me as though I weren't there. A hospital gown was given to the patient. The patient was examined, spoken to, prodded, and discussed in whispers. Curing the Patient so she may return to her true self was their only objective. There was an odd irony in all of this: I had just been diagnosed for a year, but I could barely recall what it was like to be myself.

Twenty doses of intense chemotherapy were administered to my immune system over the course of the following week, which was more chemotherapy than I had received in the year since my diagnosis. I kept my hospital room tidy during all of this. I had always like planning and arranging things, but when I piled my books, medications, and water bottles on my bedside table in rows as straight as rulers, my neatness bordered on obsessive-compulsive. Instead of putting on a medical gown, I wore my own robe, sheepskin slippers, and pajamas. I got out of bed every morning and went to my hospital room's fold-out couch, which I remade with clean covers and sheets. Bringing a portable speaker from home, I drowned out the sounds of the hospital by blasting Bach or James Brown while I edited my New York Times essays and answered emails. I worked frantically, wanting to finish as much as I could before the chemo's negative effects worsened. They inevitably did, so I carried a yellow pail of vomit under one arm as I typed.

On Day Zero, the morning of the transplant, Will and my parents showed up at my hospital room with blue face masks and yellow surgical gowns. My brother came next, greeting me as usual. He leaned over to give me a fist bump through our latex gloves and exclaimed, "Salut, Suleikemia." "I hope I never have to hear that again," I said after laughing. What humor had been in the air vanished a few minutes later as six physicians and nurses walked into the room.

After all the excitement, the actual process was a little underwhelming. My brother's stem cells were dripping from a hanging IV bag while everyone stood solemnly in two rows, guarding my bed like a regiment of soldiers. As the final droplets drained into my veins, I felt at ease—possibly because I wasn't actually there. I closed my eyes and started to picture myself walking through the streets of Tunisia after sitting at a café with Will on a different continent, across an ocean. My hair was long again, and my body was powerful.

It was finished in a matter of minutes, and everyone retreated from the room to give me time to recover.

My medical staff informed me that the days and weeks I would have to wait for Adam's cells to engraft in my marrow would be the most difficult. I was placed back in "isolation." Compared to Mount Sinai, the transplant unit's precautions were much more stringent. Any contaminants in the air were filtered out by a dedicated vent in my room. To eradicate any possible bacteria, I nuked every piece of food I ate until it was completely gone. Everyone who came into my room had to wash their hands and put on the equivalent of a hazmat suit, which included booties over their shoes, a hospital gown, plastic gloves, and a face mask. I could die from a paper cut, a kiss, a handshake, fresh produce, the common cold, or anything else until my immune system recovered. Even flowers were prohibited, but it seemed arrogant to tell friends and family about this, so bouquet deliveries piled up outside my door, unopened.

Reaching Day 100, sometimes known as "Examination Day," the first significant benchmark for assessing a patient's recuperation from the transplant, was the aim. The hours blended together as I attempted to keep track of time from my bed, where I lay for the days and nights at a 45-degree inclination to protect my lungs from filling with fluid. My IV machine, which carried my daily dose of fluids, immunosuppressants, antinausea drugs, three types of antibiotics, and a continuous flow of morphine, draped over my bed like an awning. The hiss of chilly air, a continuous, tense sound, came from the ceiling vent.

I traveled in this manner for about two weeks without any significant incidents. Then, early on Day 14, I was awakened by a deep, continuous scream that was so loud. It was dark in the room. There was a ringing alarm. I was encircled by tubes that resembled snakes. I had a smooth chest. Something dripped down my sides and spurted from beneath my collarbone. The door opened a second later, and I saw the face of a nurse. It wasn't until she clutched my shoulder that I realized I was the one screaming. "Holy shit," she exclaimed, looking down at me with dread. Dozens of insects were scuttling over me and biting at my flesh, giving me a nightmare. I had torn my catheter straight out of my chest in a drugged-out frenzy.

Around the second week of being confined in a room, a tipping point occurs, a unique form of claustrophobia that is only experienced during extended hospital stays. Time begins to lengthen; space disintegrates. You spend so many hours staring at the ceiling that you start to notice patterns and shapes, whole galaxies emerging in the popcorn plaster's nooks and crannies. You start to feel surrounded by walls. You crave it more than anything else you've ever craved before—to be outside, to feel the rain trickle down the back of your neck, to tilt your head up and taste the sky on your tongue—when the pitter-patter of rain against the glass awakens you from a pharmaceutical daze. Even though you are perfectly aware that the windows are sealed shut, you attempt to open them. Your desperation starts to veer toward insanity.

Unless they have been incarcerated, most people have no idea what it's like to live like this, confined in a little white room with no end in sight. I was frequently reminded of Lil' GQ, the death row inmate who had written to me a few weeks prior, while I was in the transplant unit. What did he do in solitary confinement for so long, I wondered? I pondered how—if—he had managed to keep his sanity intact. Partly motivated by him, I started writing a column in which I discussed what I called my "incanceration":

The prisoner's vocabulary seems to be screaming out from everywhere to a cancer patient. Your movements are tracked. Basic decisions like what to eat and when to consume it need higher-order permission. In addition, chemotherapy feels like a punishment that is almost fatal. The judge is the medical personnel. Your doctor may sentence you to home arrest, probation, long periods of "jail," or even death row, depending on the circumstances. Although I've never had to stand in court, I can only imagine how your heart races when a doctor reads the results of your biopsy.

It wasn't just Lil' GQ who kept me company during those long, dizzy days in the transplant unit with their comments. Every morning, I opened my inbox to see scores of notes from "Life, Interrupted" readers. Writing had provided me a doorway that allowed me to travel across time, space, and continents, even though I was not permitted to leave my hospital room.

Many of the persons I spoke to had experienced illness themselves. I received a message from Unique, a teenage girl in Florida who was receiving treatment for liver cancer. The majority of the communication was made up of emojis. I spoke with Howard, a retired art historian from Ohio who had spent the majority of his life dealing with an enigmatic, chronic autoimmune disease. I'm an old man, and you're a young woman. I'm looking back, and you're looking forward. The only thing we probably have in common, he argued, is our death. Nothing in the material world—dinner, jazz, beverages, conversation, or anything else—has meaning. What remains after everything else is removed is meaning. Many people I spoke with had never had illness in their lives, but they could identify to the idea of having their lives "interrupted" in a more general sense. It came from the infertile wife of a senator in the Midwest. From a bipolar young man in Boston who was living out of his car after experiencing homelessness. from Katherine, a California high school teacher who was grieving the loss of her son.

These strangers and their experiences soon became my conduits to the outside world, even though I should have felt more alone in the transplant unit than ever before. Even though I hardly ever had the stamina to reply, I enjoyed the letters I got. Since the young adults with cancer were my people, I made writing back to them my first priority when I did. One was Johnny, a Michigan boy of nineteen who was also receiving leukemia treatment at Sloan Kettering. I immediately responded to his message on Twitter when he read my essay. I had never had the chance to speak with a young person who had the same diagnosis as myself before. We were both placed on "isolation" status, kept apart in our separate Bubbles on separate floors of the same hospital, and prohibited from any in-person meetings. Instead, we conversed online, frequently ranging from the absurd to the serious in a single, long, run-on sentence. Both of us were so high on morphine that we were relieved that we didn't have to worry about language, spelling, or punctuation.

What is your favorite item from the hospital's menu, Johnny?

The QUESADILLAS, I said.

Johnny: I was ecstatic yesterday after eating a quesadilla.

Me: Do you lack patience?

Johnny: I was just transferred to the pediatric ward. The view is not as nice, and the other person has to pass past me to use the restroom because I have the middle bed.

How are you feeling following a bone marrow transplant, Johnny?

Me: irritable and grumpy. Every day at five in the morning, the nurses come in to weigh me.

Johnny: I'm really excited to be cancer-free.

Me: the same. Do you know any time-speeding spells?

I felt terrible for Johnny. Despite the brutality of our common experience, there was a strange kind of beauty between us: Two total strangers were standing there, arms reaching out from our screens and embracing each other tightly.

I lay in bed about three weeks following my transplant, or Day Plus 20, as the doctors and nurses called it, as Will stood with his back to me, staring out my hospital room window and telling me about the morning scene. Sunshine fractals on the other side of the East River. A bridge's edge protruding above charred tenement houses. Like pieces in a Monopoly game, yellow cabs dart down York Avenue. Suit-clad hustlers on their way to work. I wanted to stand with him, but I was too exhausted to drag my IV pole five feet to his location. The medicines were making my eyes heavy, but I knew he would be off to the office in a few minutes. He was gone by the time I woke up next.

Such slumber served as a sort of haven, neutralizing the transplant's side effects. My skin was bare and velvety, almost larval, and the few hairs that had returned to my body during the research experiment were falling out once more. With all the steroids and fluids being pumped into my body, my cheeks had gotten round and puffy, yet my weight had fallen and my already skeletal torso had shrunk. Cancer patients refer to this as a moon face. I felt like a monster, less moon face, and shrunken and stretched in all the wrong places, with broken blood vessels bursting across my skin like watercolor paint.

My immune system was totally destroyed. It was taking longer than I had anticipated for Adam's healthy stem cells to engraft. Adam should have been concentrating on examinations, celebrations, and graduation during his final weeks of college. However, he hid his concern behind a mask, much like my parents and everyone else who stepped inside this sterilized Bubble.

I heard my parents' voices when I woke up later that day. I felt something in my throat tear and separate like Velcro as I turned my head to greet them. I stumbled forward, heaving up a monstrous mass of flesh into the plastic bucket by my bed, my mouth swollen with blood.

"What took place?" My parents called for the nurse in a panic.

The nurse carefully surveyed the mess and stated, "Your daughter just vomited up the lining of her esophagus."

I could only eat ice chips and talk because the mucous membranes lining my throat, mouth, and gastrointestinal tract were being burned away by the chemotherapy. I spat up pieces of burnt flesh into the bucket beside my bed hour after hour. I spent most of my waking hours acting like a statue, attempting to sit still in the hopes that it would calm my seething stomach, but the pain and antinausea medications helped a little. They hooked me up to a feeding tube, a direct line to a bag of greenish-yellow liquid that looked like Mountain Dew, as soon as the doctors arrived, enclosing my bed in a protective ring of yellow medical gowns.

Will came back that night. He had come to hang out with me instead of attending a work dinner. I wanted to know about his day in detail. Did he accomplish anything noteworthy? Was he in the park for lunch? Any rumors circulating the office? However, the nurse interrupted us as she was hanging a fresh medication bag. I would quickly feel sleepy from it. Even if I was only available for a few turns, Will offered to set up the Scrabble board or read to me. I couldn't recall our most recent performance.

Will had a lot on his plate between his job and the soccer and basketball leagues he had joined the week before I went into the transplant unit. I was usually sound asleep by the time he arrived at the hospital. Like all caregivers, I understood he needed a way to deal with the stress of our position, but I couldn't figure out why he was suddenly so busy. It became increasingly apparent that we were looking at one another through diametrically opposed telescopes.

Will covered me with a hot blanket while my teeth chattered. He filled a Dixie cup with water for me. As a temporary remedy for my sore cheeks, I moistened my tongue and let the cold liquid to swirl around my mouth before spitting it out. The hand with the water bottle was not something I wanted to resent. I was at battle with my own body. We had so much to discuss, yet I was suddenly overcome with a profound sense of tiredness. Once more, my eyelids felt heavy. Will took a seat next my bed. We held hands through blue latex gloves as I fell asleep.

Chapter 7: Hope Lodge

I rolled out of the hospital in a wheelchair onto York Avenue, allowing the sun to warm my sallow face. Even though it was a warm May afternoon, I was wearing a ski jacket and a wool hat, and my teeth were chattering as usual. I waited as my mother and Will called a cab, the wheelchair jammed the crowded pavement outside the hospital's main door. Pedestrians moved aside, unintentionally watching our small procession. As I climbed into the waiting taxi, my feet briefly touched the sidewalk.

A little over a month had passed since my transplant procedure. According to the doctors, Adam's cells were finally starting to engraft in my bone marrow, even though my immune system was still nonexistent. I was making progress: I was able to walk around, albeit slowly and mostly unassisted, I had moved from a feeding tube to being able to eat a few saltine crackers, and my blood counts were gradually shifting in the right way. Day 100 was still a few weeks away, so we wouldn't know if the transplant had been successful until then, but for now, I was concentrating on a smaller win: discharge.

The Hope Lodge, a sort of halfway home for cancer patients in Midtown Manhattan, was where the doctors were sending me to spend the next three months. It was a sixty-room gray concrete structure a block from Penn Station and across the street from a Jack's 99-Cent Store. I'd have to wear a mask and gloves everywhere I went for the foreseeable future. My physicians warned me to avoid germs, public spaces, and subways. The sidewalk was packed with people as I rolled from the taxi to the door. I pulled my face mask over my mouth more tightly.

In an ideal world, I wouldn't have had to live at all, but I was thankful that a place like the Hope Lodge existed and appreciative of the kindness of the strangers who had donated the funds to open it. Ideally, I would have had a place of my own. My mother had kept onto her first flat in the East Village for many years, renting it to long-term renters until recently, and I would have moved there. However, my immune system was still too weak to live close to the dumpsters in a ground-floor flat of a prewar structure. In addition, it was too small for me to live there with my mother and Will. Soon after my transplant, it became evident that caring for a new transplant patient was a full-time job, which my mother and Will intended to share. As a kind of caregiver outpost, we had agreed that I would remain in the Hope Lodge and that they might use the flat as needed. Given the situation, it was the best approach we could devise.

As soon as we got to the Hope Lodge, it collapsed. A receptionist welcomed us inside and gave us a room key and an information booklet. After that, Will and my mother started to follow me into the elevator to the room upstairs. However, the receptionist called us to inform us that there were no exceptions to the rule that only one caregiver could accompany a patient on the residential levels at a time. We made an effort to argue that such strict procedures ignored the needs and unpredictable nature of disease. However, the rules were the rules, and it became evident that I couldn't expect Will and my mother to divide caregiving responsibilities in a way that was fluid and coordinated, like a family. No spontaneity would exist, and there would be no space for them to help me or help one another. I would be forced to choose between the two all the time.

I felt conflicted. I felt like Will and I were drifting apart, and I didn't want to be separated from him, but I wanted the kind of support that you could really only get from a parent. My biggest worry, apart from death, had been losing him from the day I was diagnosed, and now that I was more ill than ever, I felt compelled to keep him close. In order to accommodate Will's work schedule, I proposed that he reside with me at the Hope Lodge and that my mother visit throughout the day. It appeared to be a good compromise at the time.

Will and I shared a drab room at the Hope Lodge, with a brownish carpet, two twin beds, and motel furnishings, and no natural light. There was a communal kitchen down the hall, where we would run into patients and other caretakers and have to stop for small talk such, "How's the old brain tumor?" or "Just coming from the hospital?" Sadness weighed down the atmosphere in the building. Every resident of this place has left behind a true existence somewhere.

To improve the atmosphere, the Hope Lodge team put in a lot of effort. Patients could sit and socialize with friends and family in the sixth-floor living area, which featured a fireplace and a large outside terrace. Volunteers hosted special events several times a week, including comedy performances, concerts, and meals provided by nearby restaurants. lessons on subjects such as Zen meditation and neutropenic-friendly cookery lessons were also available in the lounge. A group of women from Manhattan even arranged a weekly "teatime." With their Chanel pantsuits and six-inch stilettos, they swooped down on the lounge every Wednesday afternoon to set up trays of cakes and pastries. Although I'm sure these women meant well, I couldn't stand the way they spoke to us patients in slow, loud phrases with a condescending tone, as if we weren't just ill but somehow didn't know English. Teatime quickly became something I hated. I didn't need their sympathy or generosity. I didn't want to be the week's best deed.

Sleeping for eighteen hours a day was the main part of my post-transplant regimen. When I wasn't sleeping, I laid in bed with my eyes closed because I was too tired to read, talk, or sit up. Oddly, Fifty Shades of Grey was the sole exception. In a single weekend, I breathed in the entire trilogy. It felt like science fiction since it was so out of the ordinary and so different from my world. It was the only thing that distracted me from the overwhelming nausea in a captivating, humorously awful way.

I asked Will one morning, "Classic, would you prefer?" "Read Fifty Shades or experience acute myeloid leukemia?"

Without hesitation, he responded, "Leukemia."

As he did every morning, Will was preparing me breakfast, but I seldom ever ate more than a nibble. After that, dad would give me to my mom and leave for work. The daily walk from the Hope Lodge to the hospital, where I had blood transfusions, water, magnesium, and other nutrients that the chemotherapy had destroyed, was the most feared aspect of my day. I seldom made it through the twenty-minute taxi ride across Midtown without feeling nauseous since I was always feeling queasy. A taxi driver once believed I was intoxicated and threw my mother and I out of the vehicle during a particularly severe episode of backseat vomiting. He left us on the curb and drove off before I could give an explanation.

I received an invitation to participate in an interview regarding the column on NPR's Talk of the Nation less than a week after I moved into the Hope Lodge. It was a significant day because it was my first actual outing since I got out of the hospital. My mother and I grabbed a taxi to the NPR office across from Bryant Park after I finished my IV infusions. I was giddy with anticipation because I had never been interviewed before.

I still didn't fully understand why, but ever since the column's debut, I'd been asked for interviews. In the hospital waiting room, readers started approaching me, and some even came up to me on the Manhattan sidewalks, to express their admiration for the column and their support for me. This attention was flattering, a touch overwhelming, and occasionally made me feel a little uncomfortable. I had unintentionally become a poster child for cancer.

The excitement was not felt by everyone. With Will, the column had quickly become a point of contention. He expressed concern about the impact it had on my health and bemoaned the fact that I was devoting all of my remaining energy to my job. He wasn't mistaken; I could see my ambition colliding with my physical limitations. All of the medications that had been pushed into my system had filled my brain with toxins, leaving it feeling damaged. I used to be able to recall a lot of little details, like the color of my third-grade teacher's blouse on the first day of school or whole chapters from my favorite books. However, these days, I have trouble remembering even my own phone number or the names of my closest friends. Writing had been a haven for me before the transplant, but now it usually brought tears and anguish. But even if it meant pushing my body over the limits of what was wise, I was determined to accomplish all I could while I could.

I had a low-grade fever the night before the NPR interview, and I slept under the covers the entire night, shivering, with a cough that sounded like a gnarl every few minutes. I was urged to reschedule by Will and my mother, but I declined. I had no idea how long these possibilities would last or whether I would be well enough to take advantage of them again. Nobody could dissuade me from doing the interview; I would do it regardless.

I was worn out by the time the sound check was over and I had finally settled into the recording booth at the NPR office. My voice was a weak, raspy whisper, and my hands were shaking as I sipped from a plastic cup of water. I can't remember a single thing I said, but I tried my best to respond to the host's questions and those of the people who called in. All I can recall is hitting the Cough button on the control board to muffle the sounds of my coughing phlegm as my lungs fought for breath. That button must have been pressed fifty times by me.

I was so exhausted from having to sit up straight and talk that I was slumped in my chair at the end of the interview. One last question for the host. "There are only a few seconds left," he stated. "Are you currently confronting mortality?"

I was flung. Naturally, I had spent a lot of time contemplating my mortality, but this was the first time I had ever been directly addressed this issue. The fear of death was more real and imminent than ever when it was expressed aloud on national radio. I came to the realization that everyone who read my column, including the presenter and the listeners, was presumably wondering the same thing: Would I live or die? My survival had unintentionally turned into a suspenseful drama, and people were curious about what would happen in the coming weeks. I felt uneasy with the concept. My voice sounded crepe-thin when I spoke, despite my determination to end the interview on a high note. "I have a lot of hope for the future," I said in an unconvincing whisper.

My immune system swiftly succumbed to whatever was fermenting in my lungs that day. That Mother's Day weekend, I was lying on a stretcher in the emergency department with my mother by my side, rather than having brunch and watching a movie in the Hope Lodge lounge as we had planned. My heart rate was dangerously high, and my blood pressure was bottoming out. The physicians readmitted me to the hospital in spite of my protests. Remembering my last statement from the radio broadcast, I told my mother, "I jinxed myself." "I should have mentioned that I have cautious optimism for the future."

Although we all require care from birth to death, I found it difficult to comprehend how powerless I had become. After a haze of touch-and-go days in the hospital, I returned to the Hope Lodge feeling as feeble as ever and dependent on Will and my mother like a kid. I became weaker over the next few weeks, and by Day 70, I was in need of them assistance with even the simplest things, like taking a shower and preparing a lunch. I got around in a wheelchair since I was too weak and sick to walk. My heart would beat erratically against my chest when I woke up in the middle of the night, lagging and quickening in a way that disturbed me and made me acutely conscious of my own vulnerability.

Everyone panicked when I developed a darkish rash on my forehead on Day 80. I had been warned about GVHD, a potentially fatal transplant complication, and this was the first sign of it. Hoping for the best, my doctors increased my dosage of steroids and antirejection medications while keeping a careful eye on me.

I could sense more than just my independence eroding. Will had been returning home from work later and later every night ever since he had moved into the Hope Lodge. When he called at the last minute to ask if someone could cover the nighttime shift, he would question why we didn't have more backup if I told him it could be challenging at such short notice. I was aware that the demands on my body were exhausting and that the Hope Lodge wasn't the most enjoyable location to hang around. I needed him more than ever, but I didn't have the energy to give him. Desperate to be close to him again, I soaked up his affection like a sponge when we were together. Will said it was all in my imagination when I brought up his increasing remoteness. I was still concerned.

Will texted me one evening as I was waiting for him to get home from work: I'm having drinks with some pals at a pub on Saint Marks. Would you like to attend? I looked at my phone, unsure of how to react. He might have really wanted me there, but we both knew I wouldn't be well enough to go anyplace in public for weeks, if not months. Not to mention a pub on Saint Marks, which is among the shabby and congested areas of lower Manhattan. Tears clotted my eyes as I tried to write a response. I ordered myself not to cry as I pressed my fingernails into my palms. I'm afraid I can't. I texted back, though, and I believe you are aware of that. My mom was preparing to leave for the evening by putting on her coat. She had dinner plans with a friend on this infrequent evening, and even though I knew she would have been delighted to remain with me, I didn't ask.

I was waiting for Will alone in my twin bed. The chamber was plunged into darkness as night fell, and the city lights were shining brightly outside the window. A cold, visceral dread filled my gut as the hours went by. I was too weak to travel down the hall to the shared kitchen to eat before taking the remainder of my meds, so I drank water to wash down the handful of tablets. The error of an amateur. It was nearly midnight when Will got home. I was lying on my back over a trash can, my pajamas soaked in perspiration, and the blankets surrounding me were covered in vomit. His face washed with shame as he froze at the foot of my bed. I felt two opposing feelings battling it out in my heart as he pulled me into his arms and brought me to the shower: I need you, I hate you.

The morning of Day 100 arrived. While Will made breakfast, I sat on one of the blue plastic booths in the communal kitchen. I pretended to eat, pushing a chunk of congealing oatmeal around with a spoon to please him, but my mind was elsewhere. We would depart for the hospital in a short while to get the results of the several tests and biopsies I had had throughout the previous week. There were two possible outcomes in my mind: either the transplant was successful and I would eventually be fine, or the transplant was unsuccessful and the leukemia returned, this time with the threat of death. I had never considered the idea of a third option.

While Will was doing the dishes, I nervously browsed through readers' unread emails in an attempt to find something to divert my attention. I was particularly drawn to one. "The difficulty of transitioning back" was the topic line. A picture of a young man sitting shirtless in a medical room was included to the email. He had broad, powerful shoulders and a glow that seemed to be radioactive emanating from his pink cheeks. He had a hairless, smooth head like mine, but I was impressed by his apparent confidence. I gave Will my phone so he could see the picture. Will let out a whistle. "Gosh. He's more attractive than I am. I would be concerned that you had replaced me with a cancer boyfriend if I didn't know any better.

Ned was the young man's name. His email began with a narrative. Ned had been halfway through his senior year of college in 2010, blissfully oblivious to what lay beyond graduation. He had recently begun dating a stunning woman and was occupied with completing his honors thesis. In hopes of relocating to Italy after graduation, he had applied for a Fulbright scholarship there. Then, during winter break, he had a CT scan at home in Boston, which revealed an enlarged spleen. His leukemia was verified by the doctors after additional testing. Ned has already experienced illness. As an afterthought, he disclosed that he had been diagnosed with testicular cancer three years prior. "Cancer-lite," he said; all I needed was surgery.

I was familiar with the story. I told the story. It was the tale of the innumerable other young cancer patients I had spoken to since the column's debut, stories that had reassured me and made me realize how many of us there were in the world—an invisible community, shackled to IV poles and hidden from view in hospital rooms.

However, Ned's narrative took a surprising turn after that. He added, "I know you'll be covering it soon enough, but what inspired me to write you is transitioning back to the real world, normalcy." It's been difficult for me to get back on track. After reading it, I understood that this was not a letter about childhood cancer. It dealt with what transpired after the cancer was removed. I couldn't, at least not yet, entertain the idea of living after cancer. I was still confined to the Hope Lodge, still reliant on a wheelchair for mobility, and still too ill to think about anything beyond the results of my next bone marrow biopsy, much less a life after cancer.

Will and I descended to the Hope Lodge's lobby a little while later. Together, we went outside, called a cab, and got into it, where my mother was waiting for us. I had packed a few plastic bags in case I felt ill on the drive down, but this time my stomach lurched due to stress rather than nausea. Too nervous to speak, we silently ascended to the outpatient bone marrow transplant facility in the hospital's elevator.

We were brought to a room in the rear of the facility after the receptionist called my name. I held my breath as my medical team arrived, including a nurse practitioner and my transplant doctor. The latter was sturdy, had glasses, and had a permanently serious face that belied a kind nature. "Your most recent biopsy revealed no malignant cells in your bone marrow, which is good news," he stated. "For the time being, it looks like the transplant is working, but it will take many more months and many more diagnostic days like this one before we can be certain."

"The bad news?" I inquired. Naturally, I hoped there wouldn't be any, but by this time, I was aware enough of how doctors presented these kinds of discussions to think otherwise.

The bad news is that there is a significant chance that you will relapse. Your cancer has a high chance of returning because of the genetic abnormalities in your bone marrow and the fact that we were unable to completely eradicate the leukemia prior to the transplant. As soon as you are well enough, I want you to start an experimental maintenance chemotherapy regimen.

I pressed my legs to my chest while seated on the examination table. I was overcome with hopelessness. Voices sounded far and little, as if they were underwater, and the misery was like drowning. Parts of Ned's letter from earlier that morning came to mind. What could possibly make the return to normalcy so difficult? Now I thought sourly. Normalcy is all I want. I'll be fortunate if I ever get out of these hospital quarters. My cancer was a dog from the junkyard. Even though it was walled in for the time being, it was vicious and snarling, threatening to burrow beneath the barbed wire and get away. To keep it behind the fence, I would have to put up a fierce struggle. In order to find a cure, I would need to go through additional experimental therapies and then innumerable testing over the course of months and years. Another scan would come along eventually. Next time, the biopsy.

"How long is the maintenance chemotherapy going to last?" I waited for my transplant doctor's answer as I inquired. "A long time," he murmured quietly. "An additional year, perhaps even more." I turned to face Will. He had the dejected, sunken expression of a man caught in a trap. He was not to blame. But now that I'm looking back, I realize that I did.

Chapter 8: Chronology of Freedom

For someone like me, the concept of home is illusive. I had gone to six schools across three countries by the time I was twelve. We had mostly remained in Saratoga since seventh grade, but I never felt like I belonged there—or anyplace else, for that matter. When I remained in one spot for more than a year or two, I became restless because I was worried that I would become stuck like a barnacle on a ship's hull. Because they are too white, too dark, too exotically called, and too ambiguously other to ever truly belong anyplace, mixed children are cursed to grow up between cultures and nations, creeds and customs.

No less nomadic has been life since diagnosis. Will and I had lived in hospital rooms for a total of six months in the past year. We had shared the Saratoga bedroom where I grew up. We had shared acquaintances' guest bedrooms. We had most recently been residing at the Hope Lodge, where we were only allowed to stay for a maximum of three months due to regulations. However, I was cured of my ephemeral tendencies by the end of the summer. I longed for a home more than anything else.

Will and I moved into my mother's apartment on the corner of Fourth Street and Avenue A in the East Village in late August of 2012; she had lived there when she first came to New York twenty years prior. The apartment was ours for however long we wanted to stay, provided Will and I could find the money to pay the rent, electricity, and taxes.

The building had altered a lot since my last visit, yet not much. Upon my arrival, I heard someone exclaim, "Le bébé!" and recognized Jorge, who was the nighttime doorman. He was gray and a little stooped now, but he clearly recalled the day my parents took me home from the hospital when I was a baby. The building's halls featured art deco light fixtures and false gold moldings, and all of the doors were still painted the same seafoam green. The faucets occasionally spat out rust-brown water, and the elevator broke down on a regular basis. The ground floor flat, the size of a matchbox, had windows overlooking the courtyard's trash. We got a dishrack and glasses from Will's parents, a bed frame from a friend, and bedding and a lovely antique Tunisian rug from mine. Additionally, we had searched secondhand shops for an antique steamer trunk similar to the one we had used for our dining table in Paris. We felt quite fortunate to have a home, no matter how little, poorly lit, or carelessly furnished.

Will lighted several candles and placed two plates on the trunk on the first night we were in the flat. Up until recently, I had to eat through tubes or the tiny morsels of overcooked food I could manage to eat at the Hope Lodge. The last actual, full meal I can recall being able to eat was an Easter dinner in the transplant unit. Even though I was at my lowest weight ever and had no appetite, I was determined to enjoy our first meal together in our new house. Eating half a bowl of homemade spaghetti and then struggling to keep it down all night was what it meant to be free.

In the weeks that followed, freedom also meant having patience with Will as he found it difficult to take over for my mother, who had moved back to Saratoga, and the medical personnel. He took on most of the cooking and cleaning duties around the house and went to the ER with me every few weeks when I had a new problem or another fever. The most of my days were spent by myself in bed, resting, trying to write, and numbing out with television because I was so weak that it was difficult for me to walk even one block to the drugstore. I kept track of the hours until noon, when Will would ride his bike home during his lunch break to see how I was doing and prepare me a meal before going back to work. After that, I kept track of the hours until he got home at seven. We stayed inside in the evenings because I was still not permitted to dine at restaurants, go to busy areas, or use public transit. I no longer felt as far away from him as I had in the Hope Lodge. We were both excited about the idea of moving to a new location and starting over. Being free meant sharing a bed for the first time since the transplant and adjusting to a new body that didn't seem to understand the meaning of physical intimacy.

Just after nine o'clock on a Monday morning. At every corner, someone was attempting to hail a cab as I stood outside the apartment complex. I decided to wait a few minutes for the morning commuter flow to subside, so I took a seat on the curb. No matter what I did, including skipping the shower, setting many alarms, and going to bed early the night before, I always appeared to arrive to the hospital precisely thirty minutes late after starting chemotherapy again. I wasn't in a big rush because I was almost proud of how reliable my thirty-minute lateness buffer had become. It was my time, but I arrived on schedule.

Perhaps I was also secretly hoping that I would be granted permission to take the day off if I arrived late enough. I fought the urge to undertake the maintenance chemotherapy altogether. Even though my rational mind knew why, it was more difficult for me to muster the will to endure the grueling process now that I had no blast counts—no cancer, just the possibility of its recurrence. An intravenous infusion of azacitidine, a medication I had received during the research study, was part of my new treatment plan. Every month, I would get it for five days in a row. I would then be off for three weeks. It didn't seem like much on paper. However, I had learned from experience that the time off would not be a vacation; I would work through the three weeks under the influence of the harmful chemicals, and then, as I was beginning to feel better, it would be time for another five days. For the foreseeable future, this was my life.

I waved a cab down hesitantly as it slowed. The driver was an elderly man with a strong Jamaican accent and salt-and-pepper twists. I saw a young woman riding a bike on the East River bike path as we accelerated up the FDR Drive, the expressway that runs around Manhattan's eastern tip. She appeared to be around my age, athletic, tanned, and sporting a blond ponytail that fluttered in the breeze. I considered riding a bike to the hospital one day. after I recovered sufficiently.

"Hey there? "Is anyone home?" the cabbie asked. I had been absorbed in my thoughts when we got to the hospital. "Is everything alright?" In order to gauge their reaction, I had a running joke that one day, when someone inquired about my well-being, I would launch into a monologue about my most recent cytogenetic report or biopsy findings. However, the driver was merely attempting to be kind. I was aware that he didn't really want me to describe how a bone marrow transplant can cause confusion and disarray. or that I would start acting like a public narcoleptic. Instead, I remained silent, paid the fare, and said a brief "thank you" as I got out of the taxi.

When I entered Sloan Kettering's main lobby, the well-known antiseptic smell irritated my senses. It looked like a gigantic cruise ship filled with cancer patients and their caregivers, complete with twenty stories, gleaming steel elevators, and art-lined walls. A Starbucks cart, a dining hall, the odd chamber music performance, and a recreation floor featuring arts and crafts activities and a library where patients could check out worn-out copies of Harlequin Romance novels were among its strange, downsized cruise-style facilities. Although the structure was immaculate and furnished with cutting-edge machinery, there was a certain fatigue that verged on shabbyness. The waiting areas were furnished with furniture from the 1970s, and the marbled linoleum flooring bore the marks of years of pacing by medical professionals and caregivers. Patients in wheelchairs and stretchers spilled into the hallway as the urgent care unit was constantly full.

A few days after receiving my diagnosis, I went to Sloan Kettering for the first time in order to get a second opinion. I didn't look like the other patients because of my nose ring and waist-length hair. My father has been bald since the nineties, and a middle-aged man in the waiting room with a sleeveless shirt and a bandana over his hairless head had pressed in near him. Presuming he was the one getting chemotherapy, he lifted his fist in the air. "Brother, live strong," he added. I recall feeling validated, as if the confusion proved that I wasn't supposed to be here, that I wasn't like these individuals in their varying states of decay. The patients and Sloan Kettering's sterile smell were comforting to me now. I felt comfortable and like I belonged here with my quarter-inch of duckling blond hair, which was soft as down and growing in patches. I was able to navigate the intricate network of passageways with my eyes closed, talked medicalese fluently, and knew the protocols. The outer world had become unfamiliar and perhaps a little terrifying.

I rubbed my palms together, pumped the hand sanitizer dispenser three times as part of my good luck ritual, put on a new face mask and blue latex gloves, and marched to the B elevators. When the doors to the fourth story opened, I shuddered. Like a meat locker, the outpatient bone marrow transplant facility was maintained frigid and airless. I took a seat after stealing a heated blanket from the nurses' station, where they were kept warm by an oven-like device.

Sitting in waiting rooms appeared to go on forever, and the only way to pass the time was to watch other people or remain still. I had mastered the ability to identify the many stages of patienthood throughout time: Some semi-balding fathers or sons with already low-stakes hair situations would shave their heads in solidarity, feeling that they earned a badge of honor for this sacrifice. The newly diagnosed were frequently accompanied by an entourage of friends and family members with flowers and gifts. The entourage would thin out after a few weeks. A "Chemo Buddy Duty" schedule would be created so that family members and friends could alternate going with the sufferer. After six months, the patient would be seated next to a single caregiver who was complaining about the "hellish wait times" or the parking problem due to their busy workload. It would eventually be decided that the patient could manage visiting the hospital by himself if they were unlucky enough to be ill for more than a year or two.

I had joined the latter group today for the first time since my diagnosis, but I wasn't alone. I saw a young man wearing the required mask and gloves who had just entered. He was tall and lanky, wearing a wool cap over his head, and appeared to be in his late twenties. As he looked around the packed waiting area for a seat, he appeared anxious. We exchanged nods as he walked up to the lone vacant chair, which was immediately next to me.

"You mean Suleika?" he asked, holding out a gloved hand. "I really enjoy your column." As we waited, he identified himself as Bret and told me about his losing fight with cancer and how he and his wife were thinking of leaving Chicago to come to New York City so that he might have a bone marrow transplant. After listening, I told him the pertinent details of my encounter. In addition to offering to put him in touch with the Hope Lodge, where he and his wife could live for free, I assured him that he would receive excellent care if he chose to have his transplant here. His hands were solid by the time Bret's name was called, and our conversation—our bond—gave me a sense of stability. I agreed to look him up if I ever visited Chicago, and we exchanged phone numbers. However, as he vanished behind the curtain, I found myself alone once more.

One of my favorite nurses, Abbie, was there when I was eventually summoned into the chemo suite. "Your eyes are red," she remarked, sounding a little worried. I started to say, "I'm just tired," which was somewhat accurate. Lately, I had been having trouble sleeping. I would stay up late watching movies in bed because of the insomnia caused by the large dosage of steroids I needed to combat GVHD. But I started crying uncontrollably before I could say anything more. I was astonished by the outburst. I had become a walking fountain of tears at home, but I hardly ever shed a tear in public.

Since learning that I might require additional chemotherapy, my spirit had been in turbulent waters lately—churning, restless. Freedom was learning how to take care of myself because Will was at work and my parents were back in Saratoga. It was a huge pillbox with the days of the week written on it, along with the obligation to take the several prescription drugs on schedule. Freedom was going to chemotherapy alone. It was the knowledge that I was alone myself in this. I had been, in a way, all along.

Chapter 9: The Last Good Night

We must have appeared to the policeman as two more nasty chicks with bad dispositions. We wore black leather coats that matched. I had a big tattoo of a serpent on my neck, and I had a new buzz cut and thick eyeliner. Melissa used marijuana nearly every hour these days, which caused her pupils to dilate, her hair to fall to her waist, and her fingers to be studded with a dozen silver rings.

The police officer was unaware that Melissa was wearing a wig, that my neck tattoo was a fake, and that she had just received the news that her Ewing sarcoma was fatal. The physicians had informed her earlier that week that they were at the end of their options. The prognosis was dire, but she had begun looking into clinical possibilities in an attempt to buy time. I had suggested a night out on the town to lift her spirits. After traveling to a motorbike and tattoo festival, we performed drag burlesque while dancing on our chairs beneath the disco ball's glittering lights. And now here we were, on a Coney Island subway platform, facing a police officer as the first rays of morning peeked through the darkness.

Despite having MetroCards in our wallets, we had jumped the turnstile a few minutes ago. The adage "you only live once" assumes a new significance when one is confronted with mortality. However, the policeman claimed that we had broken the law and threatened to take us to the nearby precinct. Melissa removed her wig without missing a beat, exposing her bald scalp. She told an effective lie about being in a hurry to get home so she could take her cancer medication, and her eyes welled up with tears. Her act was successful, and the officer gave us two hundred-dollar tickets, letting us off lightly. He even expressed regret for having to give us tickets at all, but he claimed he had no other option because we had been captured on camera.

After the police officer wished us well and sent us off, Melissa muttered to me, "Partners in crime."

I retorted, "Bad to the bone—literally diseased." We screamed with delight as we collapsed on top of one another as soon as the train doors closed behind us.

We had no idea that it would be our final enjoyable evening together. Seldom does one.

I went to Sloan Kettering for my second-to-last round of chemotherapy eight weeks later on a Monday morning in early March, but rather than being relieved that I was almost finished, my mind kept going back to Melissa. The tumors were vicious, and her cancer was growing through her body at a horrifying rate. Her exquisite features were distorted, one of her eyes was swollen shut, and they were pressing through her head after breaking her spine twice. Melissa claimed that she didn't want anyone to see her because she felt unattractive. She refused any guests save Max, myself, and several of her best friends.

There are some stories that people seem to gravitate toward when they envision dying. Phrases like "passed away," "being called home," and "gained her angel wings" are used in obituaries and eulogies. Death sounds so passive and serene with these euphemisms, like falling asleep in the middle of the day. They would rather believe that someone feels in some way ready when the moment arrives. With Melissa, that was not the case. Death was getting closer, and she was furious. She would say, "I'm not ready." "I still have a lot of work to do." In addition, she was afraid and kept thinking about what it would be like and how her parents would handle it.

She was an inpatient, and every day that week after I completed my infusion, I took the elevator to the eighteenth floor. She appeared to be getting worse every time I visited. I once spotted her parents in the hallway before I went into her room. As if attempting to awaken from a bad dream, her father rubbed his swollen eyes with balled fists and remarked, "The doctors keep telling us to prepare ourselves, we need to prepare ourselves."

Melissa asked me if I wanted to accompany her on a journey back to India when I saw her another day. She believed that we ought to depart immediately. With a morphine-soaked voice, she muttered, "I don't have much time." I sat in silence for a while, trying to think of something to say in response. As they sat beside my own hospital bed during the past few years, I had witnessed my friends and relatives feign cheerful smiles and avert tears. Now, struggling to do the same, I bit my lower lip to maintain my composure while staring up at the ceiling and swallowing forcefully.

"Where ought we to go first?" I inquired.

Melissa couldn't possibly get on a plane to anywhere. We nevertheless made plans for a vacation that we both knew would never happen: a trip to the Taj Mahal at dawn, the rickshaws we would take through downtown Delhi, and all the hand-painted marionettes we would purchase at the market to add to her collection. As she talked, I nodded and smiled broadly, interjecting occasionally with advice and encouraging mutterings. India was no longer a place to visit, but a symbol.

Melissa started to nod off, so I got up to depart. I bent over and gave her a hug after squeezing her hand. She sobbed as she said, "I'm not ready." I pulled up the white hospital blanket, drew the shades, and snuggled her in. I whispered, "Get some rest." "I'll see you tomorrow when I return." I took a moment to observe her sleep in the doorway.

Melissa was sent to a hospice facility in Massachusetts the following morning in order to be nearer to her home. She shared a picture on Instagram that was taken from inside the ambulance, with two frosted windows overlooking a busy street. "Goodbye, New York. I cherished you. In the caption below, she said, "My heart is broken."

She went before I had a chance to see her. I was strapped to an IV pole, a final bag of poison seeping into my veins, just as her ambulance was pulling away.

Although death never occurs at a convenient time, receiving a death sentence while still a minor is against the natural order of things. Melissa and I had learned to live with the fear of death as best we could after years of illness. Despite our best efforts, we were unable to eradicate the stink of mortality. We discussed it extensively. We even made jokes about it occasionally. Melissa stated that she hoped her funeral will be filled with tears. Together, we created a rider that included the guest list and the type of cocktails that would be served after I expressed my want for mine to have a wild after-party.

However, I couldn't have anticipated losing her in real life. In a bizarre way, we felt invincible because of how many times we had come close to death and then recovered. Even after Melissa left New York, even after she stopped responding to texts, her thoughts drifting to that other place and the watery space between the living, even after her parents wrote to say that she was surrounded by family, dozens of trinkets and doodads, and those hand-painted marionettes in her last hours, it didn't add up. Still, it doesn't add up.

I had lost the person with whom I could openly discuss everything. Where has it gone, though?

And why?

The ghost of grief comes and goes without notice. It awakens you from your slumber in the middle of the night. The glass fragments fill your chest. At a party, it stops you in the middle of your laughter to reprimand you for forgetting for a brief while. It follows you around breath for breath until it becomes a part of you.

Part Two

Chapter 10: The In-Between Place

Susan Sontag noted in Illness as Metaphor that "EVERYONE WHO IS BIRTHING HAS DUAL CITIZENSHIP, IN THE KINGDOM OF THE SICK AND THE KINGDOM OF THE WELL." "Even though we all prefer to use only the good passport, we are all eventually required to identify ourselves as citizens of that other place, at least temporarily."

I had spent much of my adult life in that other realm—the kingdom of the sick that no one wants to live in—by the time I reached my last day of chemotherapy. I had first hoped for a brief stay during which I wouldn't have to unpack my belongings. I had resisted being called a "cancer patient," thinking I could continue to be who I had been. But I had seen my former self disappear as I became ill. I had been given a patient ID number instead of my name. I had become proficient in medical jargon. Even my biological identity had changed: my DNA had undergone an irreversible mutation when my brother's stem cells engrafted in my bone marrow. Illness became the first thing people saw about me because of my port, pallor, and bald head. As the months turned into years, I did my best to fit in with the customs of this new country, made friends with the locals, and even established a career there. I had established a home there, acknowledging that I would probably never leave, even if I might stay for a long. The realm of the well, the outside world, was what had become strange and terrifying.

However, for myself and all patients, leaving the realm of the sick is the ultimate aim. On the final day of treatment, patients in many cancer wards ring a bell, a ceremonial tolling that marks a change. The unsettling and unchanging fluorescence of medical rooms must go. It's time to return to the sun.

I'm currently standing there, straddling the line between a familiar past and an uncertain future. Cancer no longer runs in my family, but it continues to influence my identity, relationships, career, and ideas. My physicians are waiting to remove my port until I'm "further out of the woods," even though my chemotherapy is over. The only thing left to consider is whether or not I will ever be able to completely return to the kingdom of the well. This portion of my trajectory cannot be guided by discharge guidelines or treatment methods. I'm going to have to find my own path forward.

Immolation was my initial, unwise, phase of recuperation. What still connects me to Will is what I wish to burn. My sadness has to be cauterized. I wish to destroy my past and make room for new development. I believe this is how I will begin again.

I fire tons of sage to drive Will's ghost out of the place. The air is swirling with thick veils of smoke. I reorganize furniture to give outdated spaces a fresh feel. I hide the framed pictures of the two of us in the drawer. I put the comforter we bought in the garbage can. I don't answer when he calls. I remove his number.

I really want to be a typical 26-year-old. I look to healthy peers for clues because I don't know what that means. My friend Stacie, a singer, asks me to see her perform at the fancy NoMad Hotel a little less than a month after Will moves out. Even when I don't feel like socializing, I make myself go. I swap my T-shirt and trousers for a dress, a stylish black dress with a high neck that hides my port. I play around with my hair, trying to make it look more punk-pixie and less post-chemo. I invite an old acquaintance who knew me long before I became ill to come at the last minute. His name is Jon, and he plays jazz.

Jon is waiting in the hotel lobby when I get there. We first connected when we were teenagers at band camp. Back then, Jon was gangly, ungainly, and so shy that he was on the verge of being silent. He had a mouth full of braces and loose, ill-fitting clothing. Since then, he has transformed. His stylish attire, virtuoso piano skills, and heavy New

Orleanian drawl combine to create a captivating presence that draws people in. He's tall and slender, dressed immaculately in leather boots and a fitted suit, and he's attractive enough to make me gasp. His dark honey-brown complexion appears radiant, and his broad shoulders, aquiline nose, and lips give him the air of a royal. I am a touch unsteady as I cross the room to welcome Jon after he catches my sight across the foyer.

Stacie soon ascends the stage in a red gown after we ride the elevator to the second floor and enter a little cabaret-style club with elaborate décor and candlelight tables. Her voice fills the gloomy room with a sensuous quality as she croons into the microphone. Jon and I are seated on a soft leather couch off to the side. We had a lot to catch up on since our last encounter, which was almost a year ago. Jon immediately inquires about my health before moving on to Will. Jon looks shocked when I tell him that we are no longer together. He remarks, "You all seemed so...solid."

"It's for the best," I answer, seeming to be indifferent to the fact that I've been on my kitchen floor for the past four weeks.

"What took place?" he queries. He seemed to be very confused.

"Our relationship suffered because of the illness," I say. Illness is the simplest excuse to use if I had to choose a culprit.

I've never had to explain any of this aloud before. I give the impression that everything is well behind us and doesn't need to be clarified. Getting over my relationship with Will will help me get over my disease, or so I like to think.

"How about you?" I ask, keen to shift the conversation. "Do you see anyone?"

"Also unmarried," he answers.

I haven't yet considered myself to be "single." Even though it's true in theory, I still feel uncertain. Unmarried. I silently mouth it. My tongue reacts strangely to the term.

According to the expression on Jon's face, this is also the first time he has ever thought about me in this way. Something is going on between us, and there is a sense of possibilities in the air. We discuss other subjects, but our exchange has become tense, and Jon appears to have abruptly gone back to being the bashful, gawky teenager he was. He asks abruptly, swaying uneasily back and forth on the couch, "What is your favorite sport?"

"What is my favorite sport?" I inquire. After a little pause, I say the first thing that comes to mind: "I guess basketball."

"Wow, I agree! That's another similarity between us! I have to giggle at Jon's sincere statement.

It feels like we are going on a blind date even though I have known Jon for half of my life. It's uncomfortable. Amazingly so. I order a cocktail, wave down the waiter, and take large swigs when it comes. I start to loosen up as the evening goes on, and Jon appears to get over his shyness. Jazz gives way to a booming bass beat, and before you know it, everyone is chatting, laughing, and dancing. We're joined by Stacie and a few girlfriends. When Jon is not looking, they continue to prod me and persuade me that it's time to start putting myself "out there" once more. I feel a little more human, even attractive, for the first time since I left the hospital.

The latest I've been out in a long time is well past midnight, yet I don't want the evening to finish. I need this emotion to follow me home, and I want it to do so. I hang out on the sidewalk with Jon. I get a shock when he bids me good night and plants a kiss on my cheek. I know deep down that I'm not in a position to entertain the possibility of anything more than friendship. It's a fleeting realization of the situation: My personal life is in disarray. My body is in disarray. I'm a complete wreck. My disease has caused a great deal of collateral damage. However, acknowledging that wreckage means facing it, and I don't feel strong enough to do so just now. After that, I am on the other side of the awareness. Perhaps it's not so horrible. Perhaps part of moving on is meeting new people. My mind will stop at nothing to evade a reckoning; it perplexes and contradicts itself until I lose the ability to tell what is real and what is not; it tells me that I'm okay while I couldn't be further from the truth.

Before long, Jon and I are speaking on the phone for hours at a time almost every night. He's traveling with his band, but a few weeks later, he comes back to the city and asks me out on a genuine date to dinner and a comedy show. He then takes me home and gives me another kiss, this one on the mouth. With someone else by my side, the idea of beginning a new life is far less daunting.

Everything about Jon appeals to me. I enjoy how his fingers pound the piano keys and his mind churns with a million possibilities. His interstellar ambition appeals to me, and it inspires me to broaden my own. I appreciate that without caffeine, alcohol, or drugs, he retains his boundless energy, balance, and sanity. Above all, though, I enjoy how I feel when I'm with him. I was a wild-maned, naughty girl when we first met, and Jon treats me like a healthy, normal, capable person. He treats me as if I've never been ill, which makes me want to play the part even though it doesn't really match how I feel or view myself. And I do for a time. I'm so good at the role that I almost fool myself into thinking it's real.

The concept that a new relationship will enable me return to the kingdom of the well more quickly is just as alluring to me as Jon, even if I can't admit it to myself. I can't get enough of him during the coming weeks. I spend a few days with him on tour. We go through unfamiliar places together, chatting for hours on end and making bashful statements on park benches. His pals and I spend the entire night out, going from jazz club to jazz club until the sun comes up. I'm desperate to show that I can hang like everyone else, so I never show how tired I am or say no.

However, I am as nervous and unsure as a lamb on our first night together at my place back in New York. Being personal with Will, who saw my body change as a result of my illness, was one thing; being intimate with a civilian, an outsider, was quite another. I feel vulnerable and uneasy as we undress. The story I've been telling is not the same as the one my body tells: The recent bouts with C. diff have caused me to lose about twenty pounds, and my ribs are visible through the thin flesh. My arms are covered in needle marks and bruises from blood draws, injections, and IV lines. Due to the numerous central venous catheters I've had over the years, I have scars all over my neck and chest. Additionally, I still have my port.

The port protrudes prominently above my right breast, a round plastic butte that is difficult to touch beneath tangled scar tissue. I'm not sure if I should tell Jon why I still have it or just hope he won't see it in the dimly lit room. He doesn't know a great deal. I'll have to discuss the incredibly erotic subjects of infertility and chemotherapy-induced menopause, among many other things, if our relationship becomes more serious. Just thinking about these discussions makes one consider celibacy. Inhale, then exhale. I'm not sure how to approach this.

Jon runs a finger from my mouth to the ring of scars on my chest and down my neck. "You're the most beautiful woman I've ever met," he adds, leaning down and softly kissing my port.

The possibility of a new life and falling in love with Jon are two things that the summer evokes. The only issue is that I'm constructing this new life on top of my previous one's deteriorating framework. Will and I decide to get together in late August after going weeks without seeing one another. We head to the roof of my building after getting iced coffee from our favorite breakfast place across the street. We take a seat at a picnic table and I say, "I have something I need to tell you."

Ever the gentleman, he responds, "Me too, but you first."

I intended to tell him about Jon when I came here. I'm not making this announcement suddenly. Will wasn't stupid; he understood that I meant Jon when I said earlier in the summer that I was considering seeing other people. I recalled Will saying, "Let me know when you've tired of your rebound," after I said that we had been hanging together. He gave the impression that he was certain it was only a passing affair. I was enraged by the comment, partly because Will didn't appear to mind as much as I had hoped and partly because so many of his presumptions about my animosity against him and my incapacity to be independent were accurate. Since then, though, what had begun as a rebound had developed into a deep connection, and I felt obligated to tell Will the truth.

I had spent the entire morning practicing in my mind, assuring myself that Will would understand if I could pick the correct words and say everything just as I wanted to. We could achieve closure, forgive one another, and perhaps even establish a friendship that would last a lifetime. But it's hard to maintain my denial when I'm seated next to Will. From his face to the floor and back again, my pupils dart. The reality? Our predicament is far more intricate than I have depicted it to be. I would want to think that we are no longer together, but we are still very much involved: Will is still the first person I want to call when I'm feeling ill, depressed, or afraid, and he is still the one listed as my "emergency contact" on all of my medical documents. However, what I'm going to tell him will make our break final and irrevocable, and I'm not sure if I want that for a second.

I mentally count down—three, two, one—in an attempt to summon the courage to speak, but my tactful, meticulously practiced justifications vanish as soon as I actually form the words. I say, "You should be aware that I'm in a serious relationship."

Will splinters his blue eyes. I am horrified at myself when I see the shock play out on his face. Denial enables you to function in a vacuum, oblivious to how your actions may affect other people or your own life. I'm sickened by the pain on his face. However, I also feel a guilty sense of satisfaction. I believe that I had been secretly hoping Will would feel a little of the hurt I did when he walked out. I want to show that I'm not the helpless, dependent ill girl that I always feel around him. I want him to know that I'm attractive to other people. More than anything, though, I want his face in all its suffering to confirm what I've been craving—that he still gives a damn.

Will doesn't say anything for a while. His eyes tighten as he gathers himself. When he does talk, he tells me that I am a coward and a traitor for abandoning us so quickly after everything he has given up. He claims that no one will ever love or care for me the way he did. In any case, he doesn't like my new relationship. He cautions that I will regret what I did when I eventually wake up. "Do you know what's amusing?" Will says. "I came here today to let you know that I'm prepared to move back in and restart our relationship. However, you have rendered that impossible.

"You dare!" I growl. "You can't abandon me when I'm ill and then suddenly come back into my life when I'm finally feeling better."

"All well, I suppose that's that. Will responds, yawning exaggeratedly and extending his arms above his head, "Good luck to you and to my replacement."

I never thought he would leave when I gave him an ultimatum, and Will never anticipated that I would move on once he did. Both of us had made fatal assumptions. However, what has already occurred cannot be reversed. We are unable to see past each other's treachery. We're both in pain, but we're pretending not to care. Each of us is too arrogant to request or offer forgiveness.

After Will leaves, I spend a lot of time on the roof. The sky, the pigeons, and the distant sirens are all confusing and unclear to me. Above all, I myself. However, I am confident of this: I cannot envision a life without Will, but I also cannot envision a future with him. Both of us must break free from codependency—from our previous roles as patient and caregiver—but I don't think we can accomplish it together, at least not anytime soon. We must part ways in order for us to create new identities.

Nevertheless, I'm astounded by how rapidly we've gone from being a couple, completely entangled and in love, to two strangers alone in our own sorrow and rage. It feels more like the start of a painful, drawn-out divorce than the last stages of a breakup as we begin to dismantle what's left of us. Will gives his copy of the keys back. We terminate our family phone plan and close our shared bank account. We organize our common possessions, and while we never ask, our individual families and friends also organize themselves.

We have decided on a shared parenting plan for Oscar, with Will having him on the weekends and me caring for him throughout the week. Will rings the doorbell and comes inside to get Oscar the first few times we do this. Then one day he sees a pair of Air Jordans in the front closet that are in men's size 13. We then meet for drop-offs in neutral territory. Will soon begins to completely miss his weekends. Eventually, he admits, It's too hard. He must begin to move on as well.

Let's move on. I can't stop thinking about this phrase: what it means, what it doesn't mean, and how to actually do it. At first, it seemed too simple, and now I'm beginning to realize that moving on is a myth—a lie you tell yourself when your life has reached an unbearable point. It's the belief that you can put up a wall between yourself and your past, that you can ignore your pain, that you can bury your great love in a new relationship, that you are one of the fortunate few who can avoid the difficult process of grieving, healing, and rebuilding, and that when it all comes back to haunt you, it won't be blood.

As summer gives way to fall, I start to get frustrated with my port, the final visible and touchable sign of cancer in my body. Until they are certain I won't use it any more, my medical staff is adamant that it remain in place. However, I want to get rid of what seems to be the last thing standing between me and normalcy so that I can wear anything I want without worrying about people ogling the strange disc that protrudes beneath my collarbone. I bring up the subject of its removal once more when I visit Sloan Kettering for my next appointment. After all, my last day of chemotherapy was five months ago. Since then, my health has been comparatively steady, but I have experienced a number of small scares, including three colonoscopies, three endoscopies, the occasional X-ray, and a bone marrow biopsy after an alarming, unexplained drop in my blood counts. My medical staff agrees after deliberating about it and arranges for me to have it taken out the following week. It is a testament to my capacity to maintain my health as well as to be healthy. I'm overjoyed.

Jon and I travel to Sloan Kettering for the procedure on a Friday in late October. I've tried to keep him away from anything medical since I know how illness can destroy a relationship. while he stays at my house, I even conceal my pillbox and take my meds while he isn't there. According to hospital regulations, someone has to be there to drive me home from surgery, but I don't ask for or expect much because I damaged my last relationship by needing too much.

I tell Jon in the waiting area, "These are the gloves and face masks." "Yes, you must wear them as well; this is to protect the other patients whose immune systems are weakened." Telling him about traditions that come naturally to me is odd. I keep watching him, examining his body language for clues that the entire cancer thing is frightening him, but Jon doesn't seem to be fazed.

Before she takes me to the surgical room, a nurse approaches and asks me a few preparatory questions. Among the routines—current drugs? fresh signs and symptoms? pain?—she surprises us with a few things: "Your last hospitalization was for C. diff and possibly GVHD of the intestines, based on the notes," she explains. Are you still feeling queasy all the time? How many times a day do you have bowel movements? How is the consistency of your stool? Still at large?

Even though I'm feeling so ashamed right now that I'm considering killing someone, Jon doesn't show it. He promises to be there when I wake up and gives me a kiss through my mask when it's time for me to be wheeled away.

Under fluorescent lights, I lie in a backless medical gown on the surgical table. I hear the surgeon exclaim, "Congratulations!" as he walks in. "I've heard that today you're being deported." Naturally, he is talking about the removal of my port, which served as the entryway for the numerous rounds of chemotherapy, antibiotics, stem cells, immunoglobulin, and blood transfusions that have been administered to me since my diagnosis. He has obviously said this statement dozens of times; it's a standard practice meant to keep patients happy. Even though the pun is questionable, this moment does feel like a formal eviction of sorts, a last step that will put me back in the kingdom of the well for good.

I am instructed to count down from ten while wearing an anesthetic mask fitted over my face. Before I fall into a deep, pharmaceutical sleep, the surgeon adds, "See you on the other side."

Forty-five minutes later, I awaken in the recovery area. When I awaken from the twilight, my nerve endings tingle and bristle. I'm not sure where I am or why Jon, not Will, is occupying the chair next to my hospital bed, and my eyes are rolling around the room like marbles as my lids flutter open. Then I remember what occurred when I notice the bandage on my chest. Rather than feeling relieved, I am devastated by the loss of my port—by the realization that I will no longer be able to see my favorite doctors and nurses as frequently, and that my trips to Sloan Kettering will become more infrequent. The melancholy is the beginning of something too complicated and uncomfortable for me to fully understand just yet. I therefore attribute it to the anesthesia's side effects.

Jon proposes that we go out to celebrate later that evening. I try to rally, but I still feel strange. We dress up and head to the Apollo Theater for a gala. People who want to talk to Jon or take selfies with him keep dragging him away from our table, even though he has become something of a celebrity among the Harlem cultural elite. I spend a large portion of the evening drinking goblets of chardonnay by myself. At one point, the bandage on my chest comes off and slides past my navel and my dress's hem before falling to the ground. I stealthily kick it behind the tablecloth's skirt while scanning the area for potential observers. My dress's fabric rubs on my raw, sensitive sutures. As I watch couples move gracefully around a dance floor with black and white checkers, I attempt to ignore the pain, but it's not enough. The margins of the room where I sit appear darker and more lonely in some way when I see these tuxedoed men and gowned women gleaming beneath a canopy of gentle white string lights. I'm shocked to find that my skin is slippery as I bring my palm to my face. Large, inky drips of mascara-laced tears trickle down my cheeks.

"What's the matter?" When Jon gets back, he exclaims in alarm. He'll ask me that question a lot over the next several months, startled to learn that the contented, self-assured, game-for-anything woman he fell in love with is an ambitious act.

In response, I say, "I'm fine."

What I want to say but can't quite put into words: My port has been taken away, but it's still there. Its absence is a new type of presence, a recognition of all the other disease-related imprints I still have to deal with. the effects of treatment on my body, mind, and soul. the cost of burying one deceased friend after another and the sadness that has been building up inside of me unchecked. the anguish of losing Will and my worry that I've erred in not bringing him back. I'm terrified and completely unsure of what to do next.

I've officially been cancer-free for three and a half years—more than four years, if you start with the itch. When I got to this point, I expected to feel triumphant and want to rejoice. Rather, it feels like the start of a fresh form of introspection. For the last fifteen hundred days, I have been working nonstop to achieve one goal: survival. I've come to the realization that I have no idea how to live now that I've survived.

One of the earliest stories in literature is the hero's journey. Like heroes, survivors have experienced unfathomable obstacles and deadly danger. They endure in spite of everything, growing stronger and more courageous as a result of their combat wounds. Once victory has been achieved, they return to the everyday world changed, wiser and more appreciative of life. I've been inundated with this story for the past few years, seeing it in get-well cards, fundraising drives, and films and books. Given how deeply ingrained these clichés have become in culture, it might be challenging to avoid using them. Not internalizing them and feeling like you have to live up to them can be much more difficult.

I try to live that story during the fall, to get back to living as victorious a life as possible. Even for my pre-illness self, I manage to drag myself to the gym in the basement of my building a couple of times a week. I get a juicer and, for a little period, make myself consume kale-based drinks that make me gag. Every morning, I attempt to write something new at the coffee shop in my neighborhood. When I go out dancing with friends, I have small moments of joy and laughing, but they pass as fast as they come.

But I keep telling myself that I should be better. After all, I am no longer seen as ill on paper. Blood tests, doctor's appointments, and calls from worried friends and family have all subsided to a trickle. I will soon be considered well enough to be removed from disability. I might even become one of the cancer survivors who are deemed "cured" if I can avoid getting cancer for a few more years. Despite everything, I have never felt more removed from the happy, healthy young woman I had intended to be.

I still take a handful of medicines every morning. My body doesn't reject my brother's bone marrow because of immunosuppressants. My weakened immune system is protected by twice-daily dosages of antiviral and antibacterial medications. Ritalin fights the persistent drowsiness and weariness that have persisted since the transplant. My thyroid, damaged by chemotherapy, responds well to levothyroxine. And my shrunken ovaries are compensated for with hormone replacements.

Even worse are the psychological effects of disease, which are difficult to treat and mostly undetectable to others. My depression imprisons me for days or even weeks at a time, like a beast. As I await the results of a regular blood test, my anxiety spikes. Every time I see a missed call from the doctor's office or notice an unexplained bruise on the back of my calf, I become terrified. Night after night while I sleep, grief still haunts me, and Melissa's Nile-green eyes keep coming back to me in my dreams.

I feel more and more dissonant between what should be and what is as I want to fit in with the well and fulfill my expectations of the survivor's path.

I've already been through so much, and I don't want to concern my parents any more with the difficulties I'm going through right now, so it feels impossible to even acknowledge this rift. The focus of my medical team is cancer, not its aftereffects. I'm conscious that many people don't get to experience the hardships of recovery, but I don't want to come out as ungrateful or, worse, disrespectful to those facing much more terrifying unknowns.

But I'm left with unsolvable issues because of the contradictions: Will my cancer return? What sort of career can I have when I have to take four-hour naps during the day and I frequently visit the ER due to a malfunctioning immune system? Readers want to know how I'm doing and hear about my life after cancer, so my editor is putting more and more pressure on me to start writing the column again. However, I can only produce lies when I sit down to write. To be able to say that Will and I are still together and that our long-delayed wedding is finally happening, that I'm now training for a marathon, reporting investigative features from far-flung locales, and that I'm having a baby—that's the kind of narrative resolution that readers and I have been hoping for for years. That would be fiction, of course.

I put the column on permanent hold because I am unable to reconcile my idealized vision of remission with the realities of my life. I manage to make ends meet by securing a few speaking engagements and accepting a part-time position with a real estate investment firm that allows me to work from home, but the employment isn't rewarding or sustainable. When I do see friends, I prepare myself for the three dreaded questions: How am I feeling? What became of me and Will? What am I going to do next? I eventually quit going out completely.

In the meantime, Jon's career is taking off. Being in a relationship with a touring artist who spends more time on the road than at home is difficult, but he has always been the hardest-working person I know, and I'm really proud of his accomplishments. I still don't feel secure in my own skin, and I crumble when I'm by myself without a caretaker or company. But I also keep a distance from Jon while he's around. He immediately starts to want for more because these contradictory messages are perplexing. He is curious about the direction of our relationship. He wants to know how I feel about getting married and having kids. He's trying to get me to talk. But the more he asks, the more distance grows between us.

I collapse into bed when Jon leaves town for a gig because I'm too tired to pretend that everything is fine. I burrow into my typical fetal position and pull the comforter over my head. I let out some harsh, heaving tears. I ignore phone calls and emails and spend days in bed like this, only getting out of my flat when the dog cries. Every night before I go to sleep, I promise myself that I will finally get it together tomorrow. I can hardly breathe when I wake up every morning because I feel so lost and depressed. I imagine being sick again when I'm at my lowest. I miss the clarity and sense of purpose I experienced during treatment—the way facing your mortality head-on refocuses your attention on what truly matters and simplifies things. I miss the atmosphere at the hospital. Everyone was broken, just like me, but I feel like an impostor here, surrounded by living people, unable to operate.

Wearing the thin, zombie appearance of someone who alternates between Earth and a darker world, I am out walking Oscar early one winter morning. I run into a man I faintly recognize from the local coffee shop where freelancers congregate as I head up Avenue A; I believe he is a novelist. He's wearing a briefcase and a tweed overcoat with leather elbow patches. I'm smoking a loosie that I paid fifty cents for at the corner bodega while still in my jammies.

He looks me up and down and says, "Wake up, princess." "Death is the final option."

Standing there in the glare of the white winter sun and his unwavering gaze makes me feel so embarrassed. After fighting for my life for the better part of my twenties, I've become so hopeless that a concerned stranger has intervened on the sidewalk. I had a single, straightforward belief during my treatment: if I live, it must be for a reason. I want a good life, an adventurous life, and a meaningful life, not simply a life. What's the point otherwise? However, I've come to the exact opposite place. I've been given the opportunity to live a decent life, but instead of doing so, I'm wasting it. My embarrassment is exacerbated by guilt since I realize how fortunate I am to be alive while so many people I care about are not. Only three of the ten young cancer friends I made during treatment remain with me.

I realize as I make my way home: I can't keep doing this. Something has to change, or perhaps everything.

Chapter 11: Reentry

I complete putting my belongings in the car and fasten my seatbelt amidst the chaos of Midtown Manhattan in the morning. Oscar is sitting in the rear, trembling so terribly that I can hear his tags clinking, and he is producing frightened, asthmatic pants. I try not to be sensitive to his fear. To be fair, neither Oscar nor I have much expertise with automobiles. Check the mirror, signal, and keep an eye out for blind spots. I recite Brian's directions as if they were a phone number I'm afraid I'll forget.

In the ignition, I turn the key. I hear the blood thumping behind my ears as the engine hums to life and I pull out into traffic. I pass an overflowing garbage can, abandoned bicycles tethered to a lamppost, and a large, wild-eyed man in ragged clothes standing in the center of the bike lane as I turn right into Ninth Avenue. He seems to be waving at me, which is a strange but unremarkable sight for New York City. The man's wave gets stronger as I drive by, his arms wildly fluttering over his head. I feel like he's trying to alert me to something. Car horns start to blare before I can think about what else. Then it hits me: I'm being honked at by the automobiles. And they're heading directly for me in their car.

On the fifth minute of my fifteen thousand-mile road trip, I find myself traveling down a one-way street in the wrong direction. I turn the wheel to the left. I forcefully press down on the accelerator. I swerve across the tarmac in a wide U-turn, just avoiding a head-on collision. My body fizzes with adrenaline as I pull over to the side of the road. As I watch the traffic speed by, I believe this road trip is a bad idea. I'm not prepared. Too inexperienced. Too weak to make it out here. Calling off the entire event is the more appropriate course of action. However, I know that I won't—I can't—even as I tell myself this. Staying would mean renouncing myself to a life of brokenness. To depart is to write a fresh narrative about oneself. There isn't really much of a choice.

The streets of Manhattan are littered with the remnants of my past. It's the city where I was born and where I almost lost my life. It's where I fell in love and where I broke down during the past year. I'm not sad to see the city go as it disappears from view in the rearview mirror.

Even though I'm only a hundred miles north, I won't arrive until dusk on the first night. I turn around and find myself traveling south on the Garden State Parkway. I make multiple poor lane changes since I'm still learning about "blind spots," which leads to additional honking and at least one driver throwing me the sour finger. Feeling overwhelmed, I make the decision to drive south and make a spontaneous lunch stop with a friend in a little Jersey Shore town before turning back onto the highway and traveling north. I make my way slowly through rush-hour traffic in Greater New York City before arriving at the verdant, lush Connecticut countryside. Although it feels that way, driving is not actually a physical activity. Grasping the wheel hurts my wrists. My neck's tendons are aching. It's hard for me to think how I'm going to endure another ninety-nine days of this, as the effort of sitting upright and paying attention to the changing variables of traffic demands a level of stamina my body still lacks.

By the time I get to Litchfield, the pine trees are beginning to filter the last of the lukewarm rays. I quickly and lightly hit my cheeks to keep myself awake. It's nearly dark when I get to the run-down farm where I'm staying. After parking under an ancient willow and stumbling out into the cool fall air, I grab a sleeping bag, dinner supplies, and a torch from the trunk. I lumber up a path that leads to a line of small cottages with a view of a field. Inside, my room is empty and drafty, with a desk, a cot wrapped in wool blankets, and a few mismatched armchairs. A friend of a friend who is out of town has volunteered to let me stay at their apartment. He left a bottle of wine and a letter asking me to settle in on the desk.

I consider making a real meal and pouring myself a glass, but I'm too exhausted, so I have a peanut butter and jelly sandwich and slide into my sleeping bag. A sliding glass door across the room overlooks the fading meadow. Night knits over everything, and I watch. As my eyes adjust, I discover nuances that I had previously missed. Trees moving in the wind, their faint silhouettes visible. One by one, the stars prickle the night sky. I try to calm my racing thoughts by counting them, but I can't fall asleep. The mattress is as hard and rugged as bedrock, making it impossible for me to feel comfortable. I find myself wondering why I'm on the road at all and what I'm doing here while I toss and turn, wishing I had my own bed. The darkness whispers various concerns into my ears as the hours pass, bringing to mind the terrible things that might occur during the coming months. My heart is racing in my chest as I stumble forward after hearing a huge bang outside the cottage, only to realize it's just the screen door that sprang loose in the wind. I lie down again, feeling like a helpless twenty-seven-year-old lady who is terrified of the dark.

Meanwhile, Oscar has remained sound sleeping the entire time. He is dozing off while snuggled up on an overstuffed armchair and makes the sound of a quiet puff, puff, pffft. I am envious of his self-assuredness and the complete trust with which he navigates the world, oblivious to the danger and death that lie within. I mumble his name, and to my relief, I hear him wake up and leap to the ground. He nuzzles his nose on my hand after loping across the room with his nails clipping the cold brick. I stroke the cot and say, "Get on up." Oscar looks up at me in confusion, knowing that he is not permitted to sleep in bed. I give the bed another pat. With an awkward thud, he lands on the mattress after flinging himself into the air while crouching low on his stumpy hindquarters. I run my fingers over the smooth fur behind his ears, down the rough neck crest, and onto his belly's pink, mottled flesh. He nestles into my chest and lets out a moan of delight. We become friends in the shadows of our makeshift camp as I put my arm around him. My T-shirt's lightweight cotton lets his warmth shine through. I shut my eyes. The next time I open eyes, I see a pale orange band rising across the meadow. The second day has arrived.

Haggard and bleary-eyed, I lock up, write a thank-you note, and plod up the hill to the car at dawn. After traveling across two-lane country roads for an hour and a half, I reach the first place on my list: Miss Porter's, an all-girls boarding school. The location appears to be from an Edith Wharton novel, with white clapboard Victorian dormitories rising from well-kept gardens. I'm looking around the walkway, nervously glancing past groups of females racing to class with bulky bags, until my gaze lands on a face that seems somewhat familiar.

It's startling to see Ned in person. I try to compare the man in front of me to the picture of the bald cancer patient sitting shirtless on the edge of a hospital bed that I got three years ago. Ned wears glasses, a blue collared shirt, and wrinkled slacks, giving him the sophisticated, literary appearance of someone much older than his twenty-nine years. He also has a full head of thick, brown hair. I find it difficult to accept that this individual was ever ill. Any sense of intimacy I had with him rapidly evaporates as he crosses the street to greet me. I understand that we are just two strangers meeting for the first time on a sidewalk, away from the cozy light of our computer displays.

I give Ned an uncomfortable hug. "I can't wait to meet you!" he replies, smiling shyly. "And so are my students!" When we were organizing my visit, he requested if I might meet with his pupils and tell them a little bit about my travels. He teaches English to tenth graders here at Miss Porter's. Oscar bounces eagerly as he walks me across campus to a shingled schoolhouse. "This way," he exclaims.

In a tiny classroom, the dozen or so girls are seated in a semicircle around a wooden table. With their long, glossy ponytails and fleece coats, they have the athletic, lithe appearance of thoroughbreds. My chest gets splotchy the way it does when I'm the center of attention, and I can feel the heat rising to my cheeks. As I look around the room,

I start to believe that a gaggle of teenage females and an online pen pal are the most scary audience there is.

Ned yells, "Good morning, ladies." "I want to introduce you to a very special visitor."

I introduce myself as Suleika Jaouad. "And this is Oscar, my dog."

Oscar's fuzzy butt starts to wap-wap-wap at the sound of his name, and he squeaks with joy. As the girls leap from their seats to pet him, a chorus of oohs fills the room, and I quietly thank Oscar for introducing himself. The focus shifts back to me after the excitement has subsided and Ned has successfully commanded the girls to return to their seats. Telling them that I'm on a lengthy road trip across the nation—a hundred days, to be exact—I sway uneasily from leg to leg. They are my first stop after leaving home yesterday.

I miss being outside in the courtyard's fresh air because the classroom feels cramped and stuffy. I take a deep breath, feeling vulnerable, and then I go on to describe how I received a leukemia diagnosis shortly after graduating from college. I declare, "I'm in remission now." "I'm using this time on the road to heal from my experiences and think about my future goals. I'll be visiting some of the people who wrote to me when I was ill over these months of travel. One of them is your teacher.

Ned goes on to tell the girls that he had a similar experience in his early twenties and felt prompted to write me a letter after reading my column. Ned turns to face me and recollects, "I remember being cooped up in a hospital room and feeling so isolated and frustrated by all the momentum I had lost." It may surprise you to learn that I often fantasized of leaving and taking my own epic road journey. However, you're doing it. And you're here now. It's a little strange.

We are stared at by the girls. They seem both softened and stunned. It looks as though Ned, a young man not much older than they are, has a life outside of school, gets sick, has heartbreak, and lives with secrets, just like them, suddenly seems less teacher-like and more approachable.

The next hour is filled with the girls raising their hands one by one and asking me dozens of questions about my writing and my road trip. As I speak, they cheerfully nod in support, which calms me down. After that, they start telling their own tales. A day student with Bangladeshi parents discusses the challenges of adjusting to different cultures at home and at school. Another discusses how much she misses her father and how he passed away suddenly. A year later, a competitive athlete with honey-colored freckles pulls me aside to discuss her own cancer diagnosis. "I would have identified as an athlete if you had asked me who I was before," she says quietly. But now that cancer has a strange effect on people, I'm not so sure. It discards all you believe to be true about yourself and who you are.

When the bell rings, a few people stay to talk. One says, "Take me with you." "I'd like to attend as well!" exclaims another. Ned and his pupils have my sincere gratitude. They've watched me in my bashful, trembling anxiety and listened to me admit that I don't know what the future holds. Nevertheless, they appear to support my goals and think my road trip will bring about something interesting and valuable. They have given me a much-needed boost, even though I don't share their confidence. Their candor has demonstrated to me what might occur when we give up all the pretense and acknowledge our doubt.

After class, Ned and I walk to the school cafeteria after dropping Oscar off at his apartment. We walk past a wall of oil paintings of austere white women who appear to have stepped directly off the Mayflower and into the pictures. These women are likely previous headmistresses. For someone like me, who spent my whole youth in public school, the regulations and customs of New England's prestigious boarding institutions are difficult to understand. This is the type of milieu Ned was born into, however. Teaching runs in his family, and he tells me about it as we eat. He grew up on the campus of the boarding school in Massachusetts where his parents were teachers. Since quitting college to get treatment, this is his first employment at Miss Porter's. His face deflates when I inquire about how things are going. He responds, "It seems to be going okay." "The administrators are pleased. However, I'm concerned that I'm not as good as the former Ned. And I feel like a phony because of that.

I inquire, "Is that the hope?" "To return to the Ned of old?"

Although it would be ideal, he admits that it is simply not feasible. He gives a headshake.

My mouth opens to speak, then shuts. What else could I possible add? What has taken me nearly a year to sort out for myself has been summed nicely by Ned. For people like us, there is no compensation, no going back to the times when our bodies were unharmed and our innocence unharmed. Recuperation is not a mild self-care binge that puts you back to where you were before your sickness. Recovery is not about preserving the past, despite what the term might imply. It's about embracing the fact that you have to permanently give up a known self in favor of a newly emerging one. It is a brutal, horrifying act of discovery.

After lunch, Ned walks me past cornfields and down to a nearby river, passing suburban streets with picket-fence yards. Despite just having known him for a few hours, I feel like I talk to him more openly than I have in the past year. I tell him everything, including Will, Melissa, Jon, and the despair that held me captive, as we ramble. I even confide in him about my smoking and my ideas about relapsing. Too embarrassed to tell anyone the truth, I've been constrained for so long by the omertà that appears to surround surviving. Knowing that Ned will sympathize and that he has gone through many of these difficulties himself is a comfort.

"So, I've been meaning to inquire: what prompted you to pay me a visit?" Ned says.

I respond, "I understand now what you wrote to me about leaving treatment and how difficult it was going to be." I say, "I know you can't go back to the person you were before cancer," after we stroll in silence for a while. However, I had hoped that by now you had returned to normalcy.

As he listens, Ned's speed slows. I bring up Sontag's kingdoms and inquire about his experience returning to the well's domain. Ned looks thrown as he tilts his head. "I wish I could tell you that I've gotten back over that barbed wire," he says. "But to be honest, I'm not sure if that's feasible."

He gives me a spinning response, and as we go along, I realize how disappointed I am. The idea that reintegration is a continuous and challenging process is typically discussed in relation to war veterans or those who have served time in prison, not with regard to those who have survived illness. Over the past year, I had hoped that Ned had returned to the realm of the well, that the concerns he had expressed in his letter had long since passed, and that he would now be able to mentor me. However, he is still figuring things out and dealing with the aftereffects of his sickness, and I suddenly realize that we might always be.

"Did you observe anything odd about my gait?" With a tiny limp in his step, Ned asks.

When we first started walking, I noticed his limp, but I didn't say anything because it didn't seem courteous.

According to Ned, his chemo treatment caused his joints to deteriorate, and he recently had both hips replaced. Because of his neuropathy and persistent discomfort, he finds it challenging to run or participate in sports. He also lives with a perpetual buzz of vigilance, ears pricked for bad news, eyes always on guard for indications that disease has re-infiltrated the plot, just like so many former patients do.

I am fully aware of this, and I follow suit. I talked to a doctor at Sloan Kettering before I left, and he told me that I had post-traumatic stress disorder, which I had always thought was only given to those who had experienced terrible, unimaginable horrors. I discovered that some traumas will not go away, causing chaos in the shape of flashbacks and triggers, nightmares and outbursts, until they are dealt with and given their rightful place. This made it easier for me to see why the horror of my cancer increased in the days after my last day of therapy rather than ending on that day: the eerie suspicion that a horrible incident might occur again at any time. I couldn't sleep because of the dreams. The panic episodes that left me gasping for breath as my knees were scraped. my reluctance to establish genuine intimacy. the guilt I felt and the embarrassment I kept inside about how this all affected others around me. The voice in my head kept saying, "Don't get too comfortable because I'll be back one day."

Acknowledging my PTSD was enlightening, but so was the potential for what psychiatrists refer to as "post-traumatic growth." My sickness has humbled, embarrassed, and educated me, providing knowledge that might have taken decades for my conceited, self-centered twenty-two-year-old self to acquire before my diagnosis. However, Hemingway's observation that "the world breaks every one and afterward many are strong at the broken places" is only accurate if you put your newly gained knowledge into practice. Ned and I haven't exactly figured out how to accomplish this, but knowing that I'm not alone gives me peace when we wrap up our stroll and head off for the afternoon.

I take Ned out to dinner later that night after getting behind the wheel. The sky grows more and more charcoal-colored as the automobile lurches along the highway. I am relieved to have someone other than Oscar as a co-pilot because I have never driven on a highway at night before. As I change lanes, Ned gives me driving tips and points me in the direction of the restaurant. By the time we get there, I'm feeling more assured, so I pull into a parking spot, get out, and begin to walk in the direction of the restaurant. Ned, however, is still motionless beside the curb. He yells after me, "I feel the need to point out that your car is parked diagonally across two spots." He's making a lot of effort not to chuckle. "It might be wise to repair it before someone calls the police on what looks to be a very drunk driver, since we're in front of a liquor store."

We proceed in the direction of the neon red Seoul B.B.Q. & Sushi sign when the car has been correctly parked. Ned takes a manila envelope out of his rucksack while we wait for the waiter to bring our appetizers. He moves it across the table with ease. Upon opening it, I discover a collection of poetry, each with a pencil annotation. During all of this, he continues, "I've discovered that poetry is a source of nourishment for me." What I read becomes the language I use to express my experience because I see it entrenched in it. Here are some of my favorites. They may relate to your current situation as well as our current situation.

Ned shuts his eyes and starts reciting a few lines from "The Layers," a poem by Stanley Kunitz.

I have lived many lives, some of which were mine, and I am not who I once was, despite adhering to some principles that I find difficult to break.

Like Ned, I've always placed a high value on reading and writing. Writing was what gave me the ability to maintain a sense of identity after my diagnosis, even as I worsened and lost the ability to identify myself in the mirror. When I had to give up a lot of control to caregivers, it gave me the appearance of control. I became a better listener and watcher of not only other people but also the subtle changes in my own body as a result of trying to put the experience into words. It gave me the confidence to stand up for myself. (My medical staff used to joke that I wrote about their mistakes in The New York Times.) I was able to transform my anguish into words by writing about it. It brought me here to visit Ned and built a community.

To say that writing saved me isn't an exaggeration, in my opinion. Whatever transpired, I managed to produce some words, even if they were only a few phrases.

aside from last year.

I'm still thinking about the poetry Ned read aloud when I go back to my hotel room. It's about the notion of a "principle of being" that permeates the past, present, and future. Ned kept inadvertently referring to himself as being divided into three personalities when we were speaking: the pre-diagnosis Ned, the sick Ned, and the recuperating Ned. It occurs to me that I do the same whenever I discuss my life. Finding a thread that connects these selves may be the difficult part. It seems like a problem that would be best solved on paper.

I open my journal for the first time in months and begin writing. I make the decision to do this every day and see where it takes me.

There are seven hundred miles of highway between Ned and the next person on my list. It might be possible for a more seasoned driver or someone with a larger energy reserve to draw from to complete the task in a straight twelve-hour shot. I'll be gone almost two weeks. I awaken in Farmington on the morning of Day 3 with a questionable itch in my throat. I've been looking forward to camping, but the forecast indicates a storm, and I seem to be getting a cold.

I pull into a campground in Middleborough, Massachusetts, and the sky is bruised with ominous purple and black clouds. I feel a drop of rain as I step outside, followed by another. It sounds awful to sleep in a tent in the rain with a dog when I'm already ill. Instead, I rent a cabin at the campground office. Overshadowed by two dozen RVs parked in long rows over a field of yellowed grass, they create a half circle in a wooded region. It is hardly the outdoor adventure I had imagined.

I settle at the outdoor picnic table after unpacking my belongings. I'm wearing pants, a sweatshirt, a black puffy jacket, and a wool hat on this first really chilly fall day. I'm looking at my map while Oscar sleeps on my lap, warming my thighs. While I'm busy planning our route north for the upcoming week, Oscar suddenly jumps down and snarls and bares his teeth at a car that has just come up to the cabin next door. Two small dogs leap out, both sporting identical pink bows. Their owners, a youthful couple in their forties, come after them and eventually approach me.

The man, who wears a silver chain around his neck and has gel-glazed hair, introduces himself as Candy. "I'm Kevin."

"Suleika," I say. "Good to meet you."

"Su-what?"

"Su-lake-uh," I say.

Kevin responds, "What the hell kind of name is that?" He lets out a hoarse bark of laughter. "You're not American, are you?"

I'm not sure if this is a joke, a racist jab, or a genuine inquiry. I laugh too, feeling a little guilty about it because I'm at a loss for words.

"Are you here alone?" Candy asks.

Without giving it any thought, I answer yes, and then I regret not telling them that my lover, Buck, is with me. He is currently hunting bison and will return at any moment with his firearms. Another notion comes right after that. To feel safe on the road, I don't need a male; all I need to do is be selective about who and how I interact with others. In this case, it means retiring to my cabin and kindly wishing my new neighbors a pleasant remainder of the day. As Candy and Kevin return to their car and, much to my relief, drive off, I observe through the screened window.

After they leave, I go back outside and fill the fire pit with logs. They're wet. It takes a few attempts before the fire finally ignites, but when it does, I am pleased to see the flames leap and lick at the cool air. Now that the rain has stopped, I cut Oscar's leash and let him go free. I stretch my arms out and rub my fingertips across the blades while I lie on my back in the wet grass. I can smell the wood smoke in my nostrils.

It's already dark when I wake up from my nap. All I can think of is that the crescent moon hanging overhead like a milky fingernail clipping. I make another peanut butter and jelly sandwich and settle down at the picnic table with the envelope of poetry Ned sent me since I'm too exhausted to use my camp stove yet again. However, the sound of crunching brambles diverts my attention before I can begin reading. I catch a glimpse of a big dog and a big man with a protruding belly wearing a plaid shirt as I squint into the woods. He is carrying an enormous blue tarp that is stuffed with—what? I think it might just be camping supplies. Alternatively, it might be a corpse. Without even saying hello, he carries his burden onto the porch of the cabin to my right. I'm uncomfortable as he sits on the steps, opens a beer, and starts downing a twelve-pack at a breakneck pace. I give up on spending a peaceful evening by the fire. I stuff the last portion of my sandwich and the poetry inside.

Although the outhouse is roughly seventy yards away and the cottage lacks plumbing, I would still like to stay till dawn. Oscar rushes between my legs and vanishes into the night when I open the bathroom door after grabbing toiletries and a flashlight before bed. I mumble, "Oscar," once and then louder. "Come on, Oscar, please." I call his name in increasing frustration as I pace up and down in the tall grass and strobe my flashlight along the edge of the woods.

"Is your dog missing?" Behind me, my tarp-dragging, beer-drinking neighbor has appeared, and I jump at the sound of his voice.

I have it under control, though.

He asks, "You need help looking?" He seems to have missed all I just stated.

I say it again with greater conviction, "I'm good," and turn to leave.

I've spent so much time in the confined realm of disease that I don't trust not only my physical safety but also the safety of the wider world. Knowing what constitutes reasonable fear and what you can and cannot trust is difficult. Even though I like Oscar, I'm not going to go out into the woods with a strange stranger to look for him. I march back to my cabin after turning. I hear a nubby tail thumping against the porch as I'm doing this. Oscar is there, as expected, with a smile on his unkempt face. I pick him up and rush out the door after saying, "I should send you back to the shelter."

My cold has gotten worse since the next morning. My head feels like it's full of wet, squelching sand, and my entire body hurts. The idea that the majority of the journey may consist of nothing more than sleepless nights, sporadic nausea, and fatigue following me across state lines is depressing. I drag myself outside to the picnic table and fiddle with the camp stove until I manage to get it to work. My neighbor and his dog reappearance while I eat breakfast, and blue flames sparkle beneath a pot of cooking porridge. The man tips his trucker hat, which is smashed over a greasy jumble of curls, and says, "Howdy." "I was not given the opportunity to introduce myself. "This is Diesel," he says, gesturing to the black Labrador at his side, "and my name is Jeff." I wanted to apologize for not being able to hear you last night because I am deaf. Today, I took care to put in my hearing aids. I'm glad you and your dog got along.

In the daylight, I can see him better. Despite his rough nails and week-old stubble on his cheeks, he has a compassionate gaze. I feel guilty since I've been the target of enough presumptions over the past few years to know better. I was once scolded by a man on a bus for not giving my seat to an elderly woman on a snowy winter day in Manhattan. I wanted to explain, but I didn't. I realize I may appear young, sir, but I'm ill and en route to chemotherapy. Instead, I blushed with embarrassment and left my seat in front of multiple sets of disapproving eyes.

"How much time have you spent camping?" I try to be nice when I ask Jeff.

"I've been sleeping in a tent for the past few weeks, but last night I moved into a cabin because of the terrible rain."

Whoa. A couple of weeks? "I'm impressed," I say. "I am also embarking on a lengthy journey."

"I suppose you could refer to this as an adventure. This is home for the time being because I had to sell my house and am having problems finding a place I can afford. Many people at the campground are in a similar situation. It's been difficult, but I won't be whining.

Jeff and I continue our conversation. He informs me about the beaches in the coastal town of Plymouth, which is nearby. He remarks, "It's really lovely over there." "You ought to look into it." I do it because it's warmer today and I don't have any other plans. I consider Jeff and Diesel as I stroll down the pebbled beach, wondering how they will fare without a place to call home throughout the winter. Ned and his students come to mind. I consider the miles of highway and the people I have not yet met. Oscar walks along the water's edge, chasing waves. As the sun descends farther and farther on the horizon, the ocean is crisscrossed by great striations of pink and orange.

— Determined to camp for real before departing Massachusetts, I look for a location to test out my tent a few days later, once the weather and my cold have both improved. I find Pines Camping Area in Salisbury after noodling up the coast. At the entryway, I park in front of the A-frame cabin. Behind the reception desk, a white helmet with permed hair bobs up. Its owner has a portable oxygen tank attached to them. On top of the counter is a pack of Marlboro Reds. "May I assist you?" she squeaks.

She gives me a map of the campground when I inquire about the availability of tent spots for the night. "Select what you want," she says. "You are alone in this place."

As I make my way past empty RVs toward the edge of the grounds, the pine trees tower over me. I hurriedly unpack and put up my tent in the last of the light. I lay out the tent's skeleton and a plastic tarp on the ground, then I step back with my arms folded, looking over my gear. How difficult is this?

I quickly obtain my answer while wrestling with the metal rods. There had been no instruction manual included with my used tent. I discard any romantic ideas of the woods as a haven from the outside world after multiple unsuccessful efforts and take out my phone, turning to a YouTube lesson. Somewhere in America, a hunter wearing a camouflage outfit with my same tent model—a Big Agnes Fly Creek—drawls directions from a woodland. I frantically attach the tarp to the poles just so, while I continue to watch and rewind.

I haven't made much progress on the map since I went home a week ago, and not much has gone according to plan. But I'm building new muscles with every challenging circumstance. I have to think that if I keep working toward my goals, I will someday become the independent, self-sufficient person I want to be—someone who camps in the woods without fear. With an exaggerated sense of success, I crawl into my tent when it has finally been set up. I uncap my pen, open my notepad, and attach a headlamp to my forehead. I'm going camping! I write. Within a tent! By myself!

Chapter 12: Written on the Skin

It's early in the morning in Detroit's Eastern Market, an industrial area. Nitasha, a young lady in her early thirties with long black locks and a witchy, ethereal aura, is the person I'm living with. She's hosting me in a spacious open loft with twenty-foot ceilings and brick walls covered in her paintings. She works as a digital marketing for a pharmacy by day, an artist by night, and a Frida Kahlo enthusiast at all times. In celebration of my Tunisian background, she was making her own harissa on the stove when I got there yesterday night. She informed me that she had first discovered me years prior by following Melissa on the internet as we tore off pieces of bread and dipped them in the hot chili paste. She remarked, "I was deeply touched by your friendship when I saw a portrait she painted of you." She is developing a proposal to use her loft as an exhibition venue for what she is referring to as "The Museum of Healing," partly motivated by our problems. It will feature pieces by regional artists examining illness, medicine, and healing.

The farmers market is just a few blocks away, and that is where we are going to start this morning. Nitasha takes me past outdoor booths that sell handmade soaps made from goat milk, lush heads of lettuce, and mason jars of pickles. She informs me about her skin disease, dermatographism, which she has had since she was eight years old, as we stroll. She understands what it's like to have constant itching: "Itching and itching." "And more itching until I wish I could unzip my own skin," she adds. Even the smallest scratches develop into half-hour-long welts.

However, Nitasha, like Frida Kahlo, has created art out of her situation. I watch as she uses her fingernail to carelessly trace a few arcs on her forearm, which thicken into red icing. She claims that she uses this method to draw on her skin, occasionally creating intricate geometric designs or writing messages, and then takes inspiration from the finished product. She tried putting rusty objects on fabric and layering the stains to make patterns that resembled flesh under a magnifying glass in an installation piece titled flesh Suit. As we leave the hipster market and start to walk along the empty streets, past warehouses and abandoned buildings, she tells me, "I see my body as an extension of my sketchbook." She laughs as she continues, "It's also useful for writing down phone numbers."

Nitasha drives me around the city later that afternoon. A tree's branches had started to grow through the walls of an abandoned house that we pass. We see abandoned lots that have been transformed into organic food homesteads by urban farmers. We stroll around the Heidelberg Project's sidewalks, a neighborhood where abandoned houses have been turned into lawn sculptures made up of piles of dolls and other odd objects, and public art pieces painted in psychedelic polka dots. We pause in front of a warehouse's brick front, which has been spray-painted in clouds of aquamarine and tangerine blue. An inscription by the artist Fel3000ft in the lower right-hand corner serves as a rallying cry for reconstruction following any disaster:

We have been viewed as a city in disrepair, a city in turmoil, and a city without hope, among other things. We have never given up, though, and we never say "die." We rise from the ashes; we are born warriors. Despite all that is thrown at us, we are a community that has faith in the future. We're Detroit!

Detroit is a city with many stories, and I think I can relate to it more than any other place so far. I'm learning to read the moods of cities. a region that was fueled by America's auto sector. During the Great Migration, tens of thousands of Black Americans settled in this area because it was both promising and marked by segregation. When automakers cut back and departed, the area almost perished, but it isn't going to die. A place where the palimpsest of a sad past is painted over the future. On skin that erupts in welts, both angry and beautiful—beautiful, yet capable of existing only in spite of wrath. And isn't it often the case that calamity forces a person to reinvent themselves?

Nitasha brings me to one last location before I depart Detroit: a psychic's shop with a sign in the window promoting tea leaf and tarot card readings. She maintains that this psychic is a genuine clairvoyant with a specialized in healing wounded souls, not a scammer. This is something I've never done before, and my rational side believes it's a waste. However, I can't help but give in to the part of me that wants to eliminate the ambiguity in my life and create the appearance that I know what will happen to me.

An incense-fogged area with shelves of crystals, oils, and herbs for sale is located beyond the small storefront. I'm led to the back by the psychic, a young man wearing acid-washed trousers and a tight T-shirt covered in rhinestones. Our faces are illuminated by the flickering light of votive candles as we sit facing one another behind a thick curtain, mine hands in his. His body starts to tremble throughout the course of the following few minutes, and his eyes roll into the back of his head as he is overcome by what I can only presume are "visions." With skepticism, I observe, already hating the crisp fifty I will have to spend at the conclusion of this.

When the psychic opens his eyes, he informs me that an ancestor—possibly an aunt—from my paternal side of the family has visited him. His lips open and close, his eyes twitching with the ferocity of a man possessed, and he tilts his head back as though taking a long gulp of water. He tells me that my aunt was terribly ill before she passed away as he opens his eyes again. He then inquires as to if I had also been ill.

Trying not to lose my temper, I respond that, yes, I have been ill and that, yes, my father had a sister named Gmar who passed away at a young age from an unexplained disease. He informs me that Gmar has tried her best to keep me safe and has worried about me for many days and nights. I am currently on a different kind of journey, one that will take me far into the unknown before I reach clarity, even while my body is safe. I get goose bumps on my arms as he talks. I pause to consider whether I gave him my name. Any further details? Did he get a hint from my short hair? Although I no longer care, I don't think so. I'm leaning forward in my chair, curious.

After laying down a deck of tarot cards on the table, the psychic asks me to make a selection. He learns more about me with every card I draw. He says, "I'm going to write a book that will take me all over the world." When he realizes that I will find it difficult to commit to a partner, he says that I will finally settle down with a woman—wait, no, a man—after a protracted period of uncertainty. He then mutters a series of incantations.

I imagine my future as a long corridor of locked doors, and with each of his predictions, a door opens and I can see farther ahead, even though I know the psychic is most likely giving me what he believes I want to hear. For me, time has thus far been measured in tiny steps—the biopsy is coming up, the doctor's visit is approaching. Imagining a future after your life has been turned upside down is a scary exercise because it involves hope, which seems hazardous. However, it begins to appear feasible as the psychic talks, as he describes the long, expansive life I'm meant to spend, as he portrays my destiny as certain.

"What else?" With my face open and naive, I question the psychic.

Raindrops trickle through the naked trees the following day. The air is heavy and damp, and the sky is a dull gray. I've always interpreted bad weather in previous locations as a sign that it's time to move on, and I'm definitely due to leave. I find it difficult to leave Detroit, though, even in the cold, with my heater on and the rain splattering on the windshield.

My thoughts drift back to my fourth and last hospital stay for C. diff. while I'm driving and planning my next destination. I have tried to forget those final days in therapy and with Will, so even though it has only been a year, I can't really remember anything. My strongest memory, however, is of an overwhelming urge to withdraw, akin to a wounded coyote leaving its pack as it knows its demise. I was unable to maintain my composure because I knew Will was getting ready to leave our flat. I didn't take any guests and sent my mother home. I pretended to be alright with everyone, but I really needed some privacy to collapse.

During that time, Bret—whom I'm currently en route to see—was an exception to the no-visitors policy. It was he who recognized me from the column and came up to me in the transplant clinic waiting area. It was my first time attending chemotherapy alone, his first time at Sloan Kettering, and the presence of another young patient reassured us both. I recall thinking how fortunate we were to be seated next to each other that day. We continued to communicate after that day, sharing medical advice, phone conversations, and sporadic emails. Even though we only crossed paths once more, I felt a stronger connection to him than I did to my friends and family. Trauma has a tendency of splitting people into two groups: those who experience it and those who do not.

When we last saw each other, Bret was getting ready to go on his own road trip. He and his wife, Aura, were returning to Chicago after his physicians deemed him stable enough to move his care to a hospital nearer to home. Giddy with potential, the two of them rushed through the door of my hospital room before they left for good. From a gas station, they got me a ridiculous headgear, a white beret with glue-on crystals and glittering netting that looked ridiculous over my short hair. I was ecstatic to see Bret doing well, and I immediately warmed up to Aura, whose brightness lit up the room and who, based on what I'd heard, deserved a gold medal in caring. Their visit lifted my spirits, but as soon as they departed, I started to feel depressed once more. The fact that they were so content together despite everything they had been through was evidence that love could endure a protracted illness. It made me wonder painfully why things didn't work out the way they did and showed me how things may have gone differently for Will and me.

I pull up to a wood-shingled Victorian in a quiet neighborhood on Chicago's South Side. Bret shows me around and tells me that they had to strain their budget a year earlier to purchase their first house. He's been working on small remodeling tasks to keep himself occupied; he recently fixed a roof leak. Although there is still a lot of work to be done, he adds they are hopeful for a baby soon. He informs me that they intend to convert the study into a nursery, and I appreciate the large bay windows and hardwood floors in the living room, dining room, and sunlit dining area. I'm impressed by how mature everything is—the way they pay their mortgage, maintain houseplants, and sip fancy coffee on the back porch. Although they are only a few years older than me, in their early thirties, they lead lifestyles that appear far more sophisticated than sleeping on couches and in campgrounds, surviving on peanut butter and jelly sandwiches and coffee from the gas station.

Aura is still employed as a social worker in public schools. Bret tells me how dedicated she is to her students, many of whom reside in impoverished, hazardous areas. When she is not assisting with her husband's care, she spends her leisure time planning protests and initiatives for educational reform. Bret remarks, "My wife works so fucking hard." "I should at least make sure she returns home to a lovely house and a delicious meal." He starts preparing a curry with cashews and chicken, opening a bottle of wine, and arranging the table for supper.

From the outside, it seems like Bret and Aura have a wonderful life, but when we all sit down to dinner, they tell me about the past year, including Bret's recent near-fatal heart attack, which was probably brought on by blood vessel damage from the radiation he received during treatment. We've both had difficulties with Bret's GVHD. With the exception of a rash that occasionally flares up on my forehead, my case has fortunately been minor and is still under control. But since we last saw one another, his condition has gotten much worse, assaulting his lungs and turning his eyes and skin a bloody red.

Bret, a former filmmaker, is currently disabled. He can't hold a camera steady because his hands shake from the immunosuppressants. When or when he will ever recover sufficiently to resume employment is uncertain. He will have to rely on his wife to provide for him both financially and physically for the foreseeable future. He wouldn't be able to live without health insurance from her employer. His tone suddenly becomes solemn as he states, "I've received so much love and support, and I want so badly to contribute to the world, but I can't."

Despite being free of the cancer that had previously afflicted him, Bret is in many respects more ill than he has ever been. As we do the dishes after supper, he admits, "I'm two years out of transplant, and I still feel like hell." I wake up at five in the morning because my hands hurt and my joints and muscles hurt. Additionally, there is so much medication in my pillbox that I am unable to close the lid. The harsh irony of medicine is as follows: Sometimes the therapies you take to improve your condition end up making you worse over time, necessitating additional care and exposing you to even more side effects and consequences. It is a frustrating pattern.

The following afternoon, Bret tells me, "I'm so fucking lucky to be alive, and I made it through the transplant and the heart attack." The windows are pelted by rain. Tina Turner is playing on the record player. We're sitting on the couch with Oscar and Hodge, their golden retriever-corgi mix. "But you know, every time something happens, it gets a little harder to get back."

He goes on after I nod and mutter "yes" in agreement. He compares it to the closing moments of a boxing bout. "Even though you're exhausted and aware that things will likely only get worse, you must find a way to keep fighting." But occasionally, I can't help but ask,

What's the point? After getting well, a lot of folks get something more deadly. Your lymphoma has returned as leukemia. Your liver is so overburdened with toxins that it will rupture at any moment.

"There is no doubt that skin cancer will develop in the future!" I interrupt, and we both chuckle.

Both Bret and I have discovered the hard way that we should prepare for terrible news because our bodies and, consequently, our lives, can collapse at any time. When we were still in therapy, we were more equipped to handle setbacks because we were ready for anything to happen. However, any kind of trust you have regained in the cosmos and your role within it is destroyed when the body repeatedly fails you. It gets more difficult each time to regain your sense of security. You don't assume structural stability after experiencing the ceiling collapse, whether due to disease or another calamity. Living on fault lines is something you have to learn.

That night, I started to consider how brittle the line separating the well from the sick is. Not everyone who lives in the wilderness of surviving is like Bret and me. The vast majority of us will spend a large portion of our lives somewhere in between these realms as we live longer and longer. These are the conditions in which we live. The notion of aiming for some idyllic, ideal condition of health? It engulfs us in perpetual discontent, a goal that is never truly achieved.

I have to learn to accept my current body and mind in order to be well.

Chapter 13: The Value of Pain

The process by which we heal is not always evident. I thought of the road journey as a chance to start again when I left home forty days ago. I believed that the more I drove, the more I would be removed from the hospital hallways where I floated down in a cotton gown while mumbling to myself under the influence of morphine; the more I would be removed from the Hope Lodge room where I waited for Will in bed with a feeling of cold dread in my stomach; and the more I would be removed from the matchbox apartment on Avenue A where we made a home—and then demolished it.

I tell myself to get over this already. Move on! However, the more time passes between Will and me, the more I think about what transpired between us. After witnessing Bret and Aura manage to prosper together—even making plans for a child—despite his persistent health issues, I feel like our relationship is falling apart even more.

These days, I see ghosts of Will everywhere I look. My pulse races when I see silhouettes of males with square jawline, floppy hair, and sapling height. I think wildly that he might actually be trout fishing on the grassy banks of a river in the Sandhills of Nebraska, where I spent a weekend camping, or he might be sitting at the Formica counter of a mom-and-pop diner in rural Iowa, gorging himself on chicken fingers and french fries. These apparitions are largely in my mind, but occasionally someone or something will call out his name without warning, and the hidden aspects of my history come to the surface as a whirling, eddying flood of anger and regret until I see nothing else. A reckoning seems inevitable since I've spent so much time attempting to erase the memory of him and of us.

Tumbleweed scuffs the road as I drive through Pine Ridge, one of the poorest Native American reservations in the nation. The terrain is bare and rocky. A sense of silence permeates the air and settles like sediment around everything, including the rusting mounds of dismembered automobiles, the pop-up trailers, and the shacks built of tarp and scrap wood. In Lead, South Dakota, the previous evening, I collided with a ponytailed biker on the floor of their living room. He suggested it was worth a visit because he used to work on this reservation. Prior to my departure, he connected me with the personnel of Thunder Valley, a community revitalization initiative on "the rez"—as he and everyone in the area refer to it.

The cold stings my face like a slap as the wind howls and hisses in Thunder Valley's empty parking lot. A young guy from the Oglala Lakota people greets me and identifies himself as the establishment's founding director. He had tawny skin covered in tattoos, a glossy black braid that runs down his back, and a baby-faced, robust build. He shakes my hand firmly and ushers me into one of the double-wides that make up Thunder Valley's headquarters. "Nick," he says.

Nick starts telling me about the work they do here as soon as we sit down at a table. Though I can't seem to concentrate, I'm intrigued by everything, including the community garden to help alleviate the lack of fresh food on the reservation and the sustainable housing pilot project that uses a straw-bale building technique. This setting is familiar, Nick is familiar, and my brain's synapses are distractingly crackling.

"Have we already met?" I cut you off.

He responds, "I was just wondering the same thing." "Remember what you said your name was?"

I recite my name, first and last, speaking more slowly as I pronounce the many vowels.

We lean forward slightly in our chairs and look at one another, searching the filing cabinets of memory for some long-lost folder. Then it makes sense. We both respond, "Will."

I still find it hard to believe. I've come all the way to Pine Ridge, Thunder Valley, to meet Nick, but I haven't been able to connect any of the dots since I've been trying so hard to shut out the past: Early in his career, Will's father, a reporter and documentary filmmaker, had covered the reservation. He had told me about the American Indian Movement, a grassroots movement that was started by Native Americans in the late 1960s after they had grown tired of being mistreated by the federal government for centuries. The movement led protests all over the nation, including a deadly shootout with two FBI agents at Pine Ridge in 1975. The only non-Native American journalist on the scene of the shootings was Will's father. When some of the bullets flew, he was outside Jumping Bull, a ranch on the southwest part of the rez. After a stray bullet struck his pickup, he squatted behind it and used a portable tape player to record everything for an NPR show.

Will had told me about going on reporting trips with his father as a child, where he had made friends with Nick and his family, back when I was just arriving in Paris and we were still in the pen buddy stage. Even an article about Nick's efforts at Thunder Valley was provided to me by him. He wrote, "We could go visit if you ever plan to be in the US for more than a week." Few individuals ever travel to this area of the country. As we were still in the early phases of courtship, I recall being much more interested in figuring out Will's use of the pronouns we and hoping that he would see this as a relationship that might go beyond the written word.

Nick and I are completely bewildered by the oddity of meeting here, today, under completely unconnected circumstances, and we both keep scratching our heads as we try to piece this all together. Will has told him everything about me, including my writing and illness, and it turns out that I'm even friends with his sister on Facebook.

"What a tiny world," Nick thinks.

"What a small world," I repeat, less in awe than unsettled by all I've erased.

"Anyway, how's Will doing?" he inquires. "A minute has passed since we last spoke."

The realization that Nick is unaware causes my shoulders to sag. I still don't know how I'm going to describe what happened to Will and me, and no matter how hard I try, I can hear the venom seeping into my voice. I can't tell it any other way, even though I know it's unfair to paint Will as the bad guy because it ignores all the ways he supported me, loved me, and fought to stay.

I attempt to sound calm as I eventually respond, "I'm not sure what he's up to these days," but the wrath is there, trembling just beneath the surface.

"Oh," replies Nick. "I didn't know you two broke up. I'm very sorry, man.

"I apologize as well." Before switching the subject, I give my eyes a single, forceful wipe with the back of my arm. I feel overexposed since the aperture is blasted too wide and the erased western skies are too large. You feel like this when you're in extremis—vulnerable and peeled back.

On the reservation, I stay the night at the Lakota Prairie Ranch Resort, a motel. My room has a tattered blanket and sticky flooring, and it faces out over a parking lot. Next to a laminated board that says, "For your convenience: PLEASE use these rags to clean spills, shoes, guns," I discover a little stack of oil-stained towels on the bathroom counter.

The next several hours are spent trying to convince myself that I am asleep when, in reality, I am thinking about Will. I lay the bedding on the floor and unfold my sleeping bag over the mattress. I recall Nick asking Will to take me to Pine Ridge for a Sun Dance, a healing ritual, following my diagnosis. How Will had chosen to go to Pine Ridge without me after my physicians informed me that I wasn't well enough to fly. How I was upset every time Will went somewhere without me. He could travel places but I couldn't, and that made it clear how different I was from him, from my friends, and from everyone else in the world who is able-bodied. Why some people suffered while others did not, why some lives were piled high with misery while others were spared, was still beyond my comprehension. It was unjust to be young and ill, to the point that at times it had seemed intolerable. I had always known that to be angry at all of this was useless—poisonous, at least in theory. I nevertheless contrasted my restrictions with other people's freedoms. I detested them because I so much desired their freedom.

I am kept awake by a fire of regret burning behind my closed eyelids. While destroying the past is simple, forgetting it is much more difficult. I can't get the first major argument Will and I ever had out of my head. Like many early conflicts, it sowed the seeds of dissension that would eventually grow into something much bigger. In a few days, we were scheduled to drive to Santa Barbara to attend the wedding of a buddy from Will's early years. I was looking forward to a change of scenery because we hadn't taken a plane since I began therapy. However, as the departure date drew nearer, it became evident that I would not be able to go unless my blood numbers miraculously improved. But I insisted that I was well enough right up until the last minute.

Will frequently had to assume the uncomfortable position of enforcer because my desperate want to engage with the world frequently impairs my judgment. He also sat me down a couple of nights prior to our scheduled departure. "I discussed it with your parents," Will murmured softly as he wrapped an arm around my shoulder and drew me close to him. We all agree that it's not safe for you to board a plane at this time, even if I really want you to come. You must rest and remain at home.

I recall feeling like I wanted to scream so badly that I wanted to tear down the heavens with my wrath. Will was right; it would be a death wish for me to board a plane in my state. Even though I knew he was only trying to protect me, I had nowhere else to vent my rage. "How dare you meet with my parents behind my back?" I jerked away from him. As if I were a child incapable of making my own judgments. As if I'm not pitiful enough. I'm going to assume that you'll go without me.

I saw this man, who had spent a summer of restless nights on a cot beside my hospital bed, who had not left my side since the diagnosis, who had not been home to see his friends or family in months, crumble. "Please don't be upset, Sus," he begged. All I need is a vacation.

"Yes? I retorted, "Well, I need one too."

I woke up the following day feeling ashamed. I was aware. I realized how crucial it is to offer caregivers the gift of time to themselves without feeling guilty. Will needed and earned a vacation, and I reminded myself that he shouldn't have to stay at home because I was too sick to go. In light of this, I made an effort to control my rage as Will departed for the wedding. However, it was difficult to stay down for very long. Regardless of how deeply buried it was, it managed to escape.

I started to smolder as images from Will's vacation started to appear on my Facebook feed over the course of the following few days. My rage grew stronger with every new photo I saw of Will and his pals having fun at the beach, playing soccer, dancing, or going out to a bar. The irrational side of me took control when I was alone in my bedroom: Perhaps Will was happy that I wasn't well enough to accompany him. He could go out as late as he wanted without me around. A girlfriend who was constantly threatening to ruin the party or halt the night because she was exhausted was a liability and a buzzkill.

Naturally, I was furious about the low blood counts that had kept me from going with him, the body that kept me in bed, the chemotherapy I would have to undergo later that week, and the prospect that my life would be finished before it had truly started. However, angering over something as vague as cancer is difficult. Before your fury veers toward a human target, you must direct its trajectory, preferably toward a canvas or a notebook, but I was unsure of how to do this at the time. I found an excuse to start a quarrel when Will called from the wedding after-party, sounding silly, carefree, and a little inebriated. I chastised him all weekend for a variety of absurd things, such as failing to call when he promised to and taking too long to reply to a text.

The main source of my rage was my worry that Will would discover what he was missing when he was out in the world. Fear that he would leave and never come back, that he would become tired of looking after me.

What I wish I had understood back then: Unbridled terror takes over and transforms you until your worst fear comes to life.

I had a high fever at the end of Will's trip and returned to the hospital, where I was admitted for what would turn out to be a multi-week stay. Will took the next aircraft and arrived to the cancer ward right out of the airport. He discovered me strapped to machines and tubes, breathing heavily, my face pale, and yet another infection leaking into my blood. He sat at my bedside, buried his face in his hands, and sobbed. "I shouldn't have gone," he declared.

Admittedly, I was secretly happy that I had become so ill during his absence. It meant that he had to shorten his trip. It meant I wasn't as alone because he was back in the Bubble with me. It indicated he would reconsider going out again. I genuinely thought that keeping him close would prevent us from becoming apart. I was really young.

I learned about the Sun Dance, a centuries-old, revered healing ritual that happens every summer, before I left Pine Ridge. It starts with a group of over a hundred guys cooperating to bring down a massive tree in a nearby woodland. They load it onto a flatbed after lowering it with a sophisticated system of harnesses, taking care to prevent the tree from striking the forest floor. The men carry the tree into the middle of Thunder Valley, a circular outdoor stadium nestled in a gulf between the mountains, after it has been safely returned to the tribe.

The tree serves as both the ceremony's material and spiritual focal point. Hundreds of "tobacco ties," or contributions of tobacco leaf wrapped in various colored cloths, adorn its branches; each hue represents a different prayer. The men fasten ropes from their chests to the trunk and puncture their skin with needles. For four days in a row, they sing, dance, and worship in the blazing sun while giving up all food and drinking very little water. Many of them collapse on the ground during this time. Hunger, dehydration, pain, and heat are not unfavorable dangers; rather, they are a necessary element of the process. The dancers feel that by mimicking death, they are able to ease the suffering of their ancestors as well as their community. It is about re-creating and honoring the cycle of life and death, not about penance or glorifying suffering. They are supposed to reenter the earth after a last cleansing ceremony, having been spiritually cleansed and strengthened for the future.

It teaches us the importance of suffering.

I'm coming to the realization that, rather than attempting to hide my suffering, I must use it as a guide to better understand who I am if I'm to make the transition from near-death to renewal. I have to face the pain of losing other people as well as the pain I've caused them as I face my history. On these long, lonely highways, I must continue to look for truths and teachers, even if—especially if—the search causes me discomfort.

The October chill turns to deadly frost somewhere between South Dakota and Wyoming, and the trees are devoid of birds. When I reach out and roll down a window, my fingers instantly become numb. The air smells gritty and damp. My thoughts start to wander as the snow starts to fall, with flakes falling here and there. Sometimes I feel like I am nothing more than recollection as I traverse the land between. I relive past events in my life, witnessing innumerable errors and terrible decisions that I can no longer change other than to gain a better understanding of what transpired.

Right now, I'm halfway through a recollection of a phone call I had with my father near the conclusion of that last hospital stay. I had just told him that I didn't think we would be getting back together and that Will was moving out. My father told me, "You are my daughter, and I love you more than anyone else." "But I don't think I could have supported you the way Will has at his age."

After we hung up, I recall feeling offended. He ought to have been angry with Will for abandoning me rather than applauding him. I was still too enraged at the time to realize my father's true intentions. I'm still trying to figure it out as I drive.

Even though I've forgiven Will for moving out, I still feel deceived on the inside. I don't talk to Will, but every now and then he will send me a random picture via text or email. It may be a picture of me laying on a gurney with an oxygen mask strapped to my face, or it could be a handwritten list of my chemotherapy drugs with instructions he wrote down in a journal. He may be saying, "Look at all I did for you," but I'm not sure if he's doing it out of nostalgia or animosity. I detest how these letters serve as a constant reminder of how much I depended on him and how much he still controls me. I get angry just thinking about it. As I drive, I sing, "Fuck you, fuck you, fuck you." I want him to quit pointing the finger at me for his problems. I tell myself, "I want him to apologize for the ways he hurt me so that I can finally stop being angry."

The horizon is serrated by the Tetons. I'm too preoccupied with my thoughts to notice my surroundings when I turn onto the John D. Rockefeller Jr. Memorial Parkway, a magnificent section of highway that leads to Yellowstone National Park. I realize that I am now twenty-seven years old, the same age Will was when I became ill. The five-year age gap between us had seemed enormous at the time, as it does when you're twenty-two and every year of life feels like ten. I used to call Will in jest while we lived in Paris, mon vieux.

I try to think about what I would do if I were in Will's shoes right now as I drive through what has turned into a swirling snow mist. I make an effort to picture myself supporting someone I've only been seeing for a few months after they were recently given a fatal diagnosis. I make an effort to picture myself packing my things, taking a plane to a little town I've never been to before, and moving in with his parents; spending months of my life sleeping on a hospital cot; declining job promotions when the majority of my peers are concentrating on advancing their professions. I try to think about how I would handle holding his rage inside of me. While I'm shopping for an engagement ring, I try to keep in mind that the person I love could not live. I struggle when I attempt to see myself doing all of this. I am unable to. I don't think I could accomplish even a small portion of what Will did for me.

The fact is that my wants were so loud that I was unable to hear Will's. I required continual confirmation that my demands weren't excessive.

I prevented him from taking the breaks he so sorely needed when my needs did become too great. When he had gone to the ER with me on another occasion in those last months, the expression on his face had been one of worn-out duty. I interpreted this as proof that I was a burden all right and that he was waiting to get out. But ultimately, I was the one who had pushed him away, not the illness. For years, I had been pushing him away in many small ways, challenging him to go until he eventually did.

I mutter into the darkness, "I'm so sorry."

My windshield wipers are working extra hard now that the snow is falling more heavily. I consider going to bed and staying in a motel until the storm passes, but I'm afraid that the longer I put off this portion of my trip west, the worse the driving conditions will get. I make the decision to keep going until I cross the Montana state boundary. My tires make tracks in the clean, new powder, and there are no other cars to be seen. Everything sparkles in that cold, blue light as the ponderosa trees that line the roadway sag beneath the weight of the snow and their limbs drip with icicles.

What's remained of my rage at Will evaporates throughout the course of the following hour. Instead, I can express what rage has prevented me from doing, and I have a lot to say. Will supported me when it mattered most, even if he might not have been there for me in the end. I would like to beg his pardon. I want to express my longing for him.

I would call Will from the road right now if this were a movie. It's possible that we will eventually discover each other again. However, this isn't a film. When we last spoke, Will was working as an editor for a sports website. I've heard that he's in a new relationship and that they're getting along well. To love Will today is to cherish our memories together without giving in to their allure. The goal is to avoid answering the phone. It will allow him the room he needs to take back his life. It's to do the most difficult thing. to release him.

I go through a blink-and-you-miss-it type of town on the side of the highway as I get closer to the Montana border. Other than a single automobile following me, the major road is deserted. The automobile follows at an uncomfortable close distance, scooting up over the next few blocks. I'm too preoccupied with my thoughts to observe the red light beam swirling from its roof through the snow. I don't realize I'm being followed by a police car until I hear the siren's beep-beep warning.

My previous driving teacher, Brian, neglected to mention this in our lessons, and I've never been pulled over. Flustered, I park and swerve to the side of the road. In a rather stupid attempt to appear compliant, I open the door, assuming I'll meet the policeman halfway between our two vehicles. But as soon as my boot hits the icy ground, I realize I've made a serious mistake that may mean the difference between life and death for others who don't have my privileges or look like me.

"Return to the car!" the officer yells. "GET INTO THE VEHICLE AGAIN."

I slam the car door shut and duck inside, terrified. I'm hissing at Oscar to stop barking so loudly when the police shows up and taps the window with his gloved knuckles.

As the glass drops, I apologize. "I believed we were meant to meet outside the vehicle. I explain foolishly, breathing heavily, "I thought it was the polite thing to do."

The officer is boyish and has a spray of pimples over his cheeks, but his face isn't exactly welcoming. He looks down at me and says, "Never do that again." "Are you aware of the reason I stopped you?

"No, sir."

"You exceeded the speed limit by five miles."

I start to apologize once more, but the officer silences me by raising his palm. "Registration and licensing."

I rummage through the glove compartment, which is filled with random documents, maps, ChapSticks, and, strangely enough, a kid's Slinky.

Pointing, the officer states, "That's it right there."

After a few minutes, the officer comes back with my registration and license while looking down at me via the open window. He wants to know how I went into Wyoming as a new driver with a car that had New York license plates and why it was registered in someone else's name, among other things.

I begin by rambling on about kingdoms, cancer, a hundred-day road journey, and my friend who lent me the car. "Actually, it's a funny story," I say. I can't tell if I'm making sense because I'm so high on adrenaline.

"All right, miss. "Take it easy," he advises. He stifles a smile, the corners of his mouth quivering. He says, "I'll give you a warning and let you go." But let me clarify this. You just started driving. Your friend's automobile is yours to borrow. You're traveling by car.

Every time he repeats a phrase, I nod.

"But why on earth are you driving in the middle of a blizzard, for heaven's sake?"

Chapter 14: Homegoing

Oscar and I sleep like conjoined twins, huddled inside the tent under heavy snowfall. Day 66 begins with me waking up in a campground outside the Grand Canyon. As I get up and start my stove with numb fingers, shivering while brewing coffee, a feeling of longing permeates my body. As I load my luggage back into the car and pack up my tent for the hundredth time, it follows me. It gets more intense over the course of the following few days as I travel throughout the Southwest's Martian landscapes and spend my first Hanukkah at a Twitter friend's house in Tijeras, New Mexico. I become a little depressed when I go alone down Santa Fe's cold streets, with the sidewalks crowded with families shopping for the holidays and the businesses adorned with pine garlands.

After a while, I realize that I want to go home for the first time since I struck the road. I'm ready to return home. The ache that turns into a mental chant as I drive is, "I want to go home." But where is home? The idea feels flimsy and weightless as it floats around in my thoughts since I don't have a career, a family of my own, or a mortgage waiting for me. Nothing is guaranteed after that, but I have to be in New York City by Day 100 to visit my medical team and return the automobile to my friend. I feel more pressure to make the most of these last few miles, to look for answers in the people and places I encounter.

Into Texas I drive past sagebrush clumps and past lone border patrol posts until I arrive in Marfa, a dusty, one-stoplight hamlet in the center of the Chihuahuan Desert that has gained notoriety in recent decades as a destination for art and, more lately, Instagram enthusiasts. Although Marfa is only supposed to be a stopover, I find myself drawn to this strange area and its people—a mix of ranchers, writers, and painters—and end up staying for a while. I make friends with a variety of people over the course of the next three days, including a Texan heiress who lets me stay in her bungalow's spare bedroom, a group of high school drama club students whose play I attend one evening, and two antique dealers wearing combat boots that I meet while on a museum tour and who invite me back to their trailer for a deadly mescal cocktail. As a woman traveling alone, I feel like what Gloria Steinem called a "celestial bartender": People want me to participate in their family customs, invite me into their houses, reveal secrets with me that they wouldn't tell a psychiatrist, and send me off with handmade pies.

I meet a couple my age outside the public library on my last morning in Marfa, and they catch my attention. Before introducing themselves, they tell me, "We call her Sunshine," and show me their 1976 Volkswagen camper van. Sunshine appears to be just as young and carefree as her owners, even though she is almost fifty years old. She is tangerine orange, with a dashboard embellished with feathers and windows draped with curtains made from a hip flower fabric. She has a makeshift kitchen, two bedrooms, and secret storage spaces.

"Do you make kombucha?" I ask, indicating a huge jug of bubbly amber liquid that is tucked in between the front seats.

"I can show you the way. "It's very simple and beneficial for you," the young lady, who goes by Kit, explains. She has an elfin charm, with wildflowers interwoven among her golden curls and vivid blue eyes. Her boyfriend JR, who has the big shoulders of a linebacker and a ponytail, is working on Sunshine's engine. They are both really attractive and deeply tanned. They inform me that they have been living in the van for the past three years.

Sunshine and her people immediately capture my heart. I'm curious about every aspect of their life. Where they have been. the people they've met and the things they've witnessed. How do they earn a living? How did they end up living in this orange bus?

Kit and JR tell me, "It was love at first gear." For a few months, the van had been parked at a lot across the street from Kit's school, Appalachian State University, which was located in the mountains of North Carolina. The couple, who had been dating since high school, purchased the van for $5,000 after graduating, moved into a small studio apartment in Venice Beach, and found work: he was a videographer for a surfing website, and she worked as a waiter at a wine bar. They made the snap decision to give up their jobs, give up their apartments, and attempt living on the road because they were fed up with the city and dissatisfied with the long hours they worked. Sunshine evolved become a way of life and an attitude rather than just a temporary residence. They began traveling to the most isolated regions of the nation after being released from the oppression of the nine-to-five schedule.

When I inquire how they manage to keep their gas tank filled, JR responds, "We travel with the agricultural seasons." We barely make ends meet, and we spend a month or two working as migrant laborers and farmhands whenever we need money. We have done everything from digging ditches to haying horses, dairy farming, and fruit picking.

Kit and JR camp in national parks, woodlands, redwood groves, and deserts rather than paying rent. They prepare all of their meals from scratch, take baths in rivers and hot springs, and consume foods that they have foraged for from the ground. They work on a variety of artistic endeavors during the day when they aren't milking goats, picking peaches, or climbing mountains. JR keeps his hands occupied with woodworking and taking pictures. Sunshine has also turned into somewhat of an amateur mechanic due to his advanced age. During the day, Kit studies metaphysics, cooks, and observes birds. The two of them work together to create small zines about their trips, and she enjoys writing and drawing cartoons.

The fact that JR and Kit have managed to turn this temporary situation into a permanent way of life is impressive. They appear to have found a purpose in the boundless promise of the open road, despite the traditional standards of success and social expectations. They seem to me evidence that home need not be a location or a line of work, and that I may find it wherever I go.

As Kit replenishes our kombucha jars, JR uses a wooden cutting board to cut up a loaf of farm bread, a block of cheese, and some apples. Mikey, a happy surfer with straw-like hair who is going with them for the week, joins us as we eat a snack in the rear of Sunshine. As we eat, they announce, "We're going to Big Bend National Park." "Why don't you accompany us so we can spend the night in camps?"

I make a fast calculation in my head. I've already stayed in Marfa longer than I had intended. Today, I am scheduled to drive to Austin. An scary amount of time will be spent behind the wheel over the next four days, but Big Bend is out of the way, a hundred miles south.

"Definitely," I reply.

Sunshine is in the front of our two-person caravan, and my mud-splattered Subaru follows closely behind. We chug along all day. Since Sunshine can only go fifty-five miles per hour, my new buddies and I avoid the highway and don't use GPS. Rather, we stay on the tiny country roads that wind into nowhere and go to areas that seem unspoiled by society. They are extremely inefficient travelers who stop to investigate anything that piques their interest. They may remain for several days or even weeks if they enjoy their environment.

A few hours later, the emerald-hued ribbon that divides Mexico and Texas, the Rio Grande, emerges. On a promontory with a view of the river valley, we get off the main road and bounce along a dirt lane before grinding to a stop. This afternoon, as we scramble down boulders and trudge through the heat to the water's edge, the cracked copper earth, the endless blue sky, and the ragged ravine that descends to a sea of rippling gold grass all feel like they belong to us. We haven't seen anyone in hours, with the exception of a few roadrunners and a small family of javelinas scuttling through the underbrush. My new pals leap into the water after taking off their clothes. It's too hot outside to be self-conscious about ugly scars and awkward contours, so I pause for a second before doing the same. The river is cool and viscous as I wade in, and as the four of us scream and splash around, kicking up silt, its color and consistency change to that of chocolate milk. Snoutfirst, even Oscar, who has never been a good swimmer, dives in.

We travel off-road for a little while farther as the sun sets, arriving at a remote clearing at the foot of a mountain with red-striated cliff sides. I assist Kit in cooking dinner on their Coleman stove, which has two burners, while JR and Mikey go out to gather wood for a fire. She finds a dusty bottle of wine they've been putting away for a special occasion after searching through one of the storage boxes. Oscar is tucked out at our feet as we huddle together on the backseats for dinner as dusk descends over our tiny camp like soot. As we balance bowls on our knees and dip chunks of bread into a flavorful stew while the van's side doors are thrown open onto a roaring fire, we talk about everything from idle theory—the idea that our lives should be less hectic and more leisurely, with days like this—to the best frequency to wash our hair.

I bid my new friends good night at around midnight. I stumble toward my car in the dark, exhausted and sunburned. I move all of my equipment into the front seats and fold down the back ones since I'm too exhausted to put up my tent. I spread a sleeping bag and blankets on top of a foam camping mat in the vacant cargo area. I'm happy to report that my makeshift bed is actually pretty cozy and that I have just enough space to spread my legs out. A pleasant breeze blows over me when the hatchback opens and all the windows are rolled down. Except for the distant yips and howls of coyotes and the quivering of juniper trees, everything is silent. There are more stars in the night sky than I have ever seen in my entire life.

I recall a time when all I desired was what I currently have as I look up at the Milky Way. I needed to think that there was a more authentic, expansive, and satisfying version of my life out there when I sat on the kitchen floor of my former apartment, feeling sicker than I had ever felt and with my heart broken into ten thousand tiny pieces. Being a martyr, defined by the worst things that had ever occurred to me, was not something I wanted to do. I had to have faith that you could remove the bars and regain your freedom when your life had turned into a cage. I repeatedly convinced myself that I could change the path of my becoming until I finally believed what I was saying.

In order to have a clear view of the Big Dipper flashing down at me, I wriggle over in my sleeping bag with my head resting on the back bumper and my toes pointing toward the steering wheel. I saw a shooting star in a matter of seconds. Then another. I'll soon see too many to count. A warm, ecstatic feeling that I can only describe as ecstasy permeates my bones as I watch the sky sizzle and flash. I'm alive and in the best possible health. I am taking charge of the life that has been entrusted to me. I have never felt more at home within myself as I do tonight.

However, as soon as I close my eyes, my vision shifts inward and I can no longer see the shooting stars. I'm once again mentally reliving the same old incidents. The final encounter between Will and me. A few weeks before to my road trip, it was a suffocatingly hot summer night. I recall wishing that enough time had gone by for us to come to a peace accord of some kind. The exchange had begun amicably enough, but a few hours later we found ourselves throwing accusations on the pavement in front of an East Village bar. Our only agreement before we parted ways was that it would be best if we never spoke or saw one another again.

My chest gets more and more constricted. I want to be freed from the things that are holding me back. I seek simple happiness. I now realize, however, that I was waiting for approval—from Melissa, Will, and all the other individuals who have vanished from my life—before I could feel at peace. I wish for their blessings to go on, dream of a new future, and fall in love once more. I'm constantly looking for a sign or confirmation that it's acceptable to go for whole days without thinking about them—that forgetting a little bit is essential if I'm going to survive. I've come to the realization that no matter how many times I apologize, repent, or make sacrifices, I may never feel like my issues—with the living or the dead—are completely settled.

I have breakfast with the van occupants the following morning, and we say our goodbyes and promise to stay in touch. In the days that follow, I pass prickly pear cactus woods, dead towns, and massive billboards along the side of the road that read things like Where BBQ lovers beef up. After passing through Austin, I wander around a swimming hole with water so clear it appears to be chlorinated. I continue eastward throughout Texas, following endless highways until they all seem to melt together. I arrive at the Best Western parking lot on Highway 59 in Livingston, an eerie strip of fast-food joints and chain businesses close to the Louisiana border, in the early evening. I'm given a room key by the receptionist, a woman with pink artificial nails and a candy-cane sweater. She says, "Enjoy your stay, sweetheart."

The Best Western is the least expensive hotel I could locate, and it's within a ten-minute drive from the prison, so that's why I picked it. I'm going to see Lil' GQ, the prisoner who was among the first strangers to write to me, tomorrow morning. I was given what is known as a "special visit," which consists of two four-hour visits spaced out over two days and is often designated for close friends and family. Normally, offenders are only permitted a two-hour visit per week. I nibble my cuticles at the thought of spending eight hours with Lil' GQ now that I'm here. Talking to someone for eight hours seems like a long time, especially if that person is a stranger who has been on execution row for the past fourteen years.

I read the first letter Lil' GQ ever sent me in my room on the second floor of the Best Western. It brought back the confusion I had experienced in my hospital bed as I attempted to picture him in a prison cell on the other side of the nation. I had been thinking about him a lot throughout those protracted, frustrating stays in the Bubble. I was curious about his activities while he was alone. I would like to know how you move forward after your life as you know it ends. How can you face your past's ghosts? When the future is dreadfully uncertain, how do you live in the present?

The parking lot is visible from my room. From the window, I can see my car, which is so dirty and covered in a thick layer of dust that it appears to have been in a collision. I still have a few things to pull out of the trunk before going to bed, and it's becoming late. After putting on my boots and going outside, I see some men waiting near a few pickup trucks as I cross the parking lot. My gut tells me to turn around and head back inside because of something about the males that makes me pause. This is the same innate unease I experienced during my first week of traveling, at the campground in Massachusetts, when I saw my tarp-dragging neighbor Jeff and his dog come out of the woods. Naturally, Jeff proved to be not only harmless but also a really pleasant man. I ignore the warning signs in my thoughts because of him and all the other times I've worried over nothing and subsequently felt foolish.

I hear a low, throaty wolf whistle cutting through the darkness while I search the hatchback for a tube of toothpaste and some food for Oscar. One of the males yells, "Come on over here and talk to us for a minute." He and his pals are ignored by me. They're simply playing around, I assure myself. He goes on, "You alone?" and the others laugh—too loudly, which indicates to me that they've had a few drinks. I lock the trunk and gather the remainder of my belongings while keeping my head down. The man separates from the group and swaggers toward me as I walk toward the hotel's side entrance, which is the one nearest to my car. I pick up my pace as the alarms in my mind grow louder. I convince myself that I'm almost there, but when I get to the door, it won't move. I see as I twitch the handle that it's one of those magnetically locked doors that you must swipe your room key across to unlock. The man's footsteps are getting closer, and as I look up, a sneer appears on his bloated, beery face.

He coos, candidly evaluating my body, "Hey baby." "Don't be afraid." As I rummage through my bag and unintentionally dump some of its contents over the pavement, panic takes control and causes my actions to become awkward. An old couple emerges on the other side of the door as I squat on the floor, fumbling for my key. The man takes a step back and disappears into the parking lot's darkness as they push it open. The hair on my arms stands on end as I snatch up my suitcase and duck into the hallway.

I tell myself to get a grip as I return to the security of my chamber, the door dead-bolted and shut behind me, my heart hammering hard against my chest. Reminding myself that Lil' GQ had been at the top of my list of individuals I wanted to see, I try to recall why I've come to this desolate location. I had to set up an internet account with a company that lets you purchase digital stamps and send letters to prisoners across the nation in order to get in touch with him. I was unsure at the moment whether Lil' GQ was still on death row or whether he would remember me. I recall excitedly checking my email every day in the weeks before my departure in the hopes of receiving a response. I followed up via the company's website after two weeks of radio silence, but I never heard back. When it finally occurred to me that I had neglected to provide a return address, I realized that I had foolishly assumed that since I could send Lil' GQ electronic communications, he could also send them back—something he obviously couldn't do because he wasn't permitted access to a computer.

I wrote to Lil' GQ a third time, telling him how to get in touch with me. He immediately addressed me a letter expressing his excitement at the thought of meeting me in person and his joy at hearing that I had survived. It would be an understatement to say that I was taken aback by your message. The truth is, I had completely forgotten about the letter I wrote you because I assumed you had read it and thrown it away. In order to better get to know one another, Lil' GQ asked if we may keep in touch before our visit. We had to be resourceful to stay in contact because I was making up a lot of my itinerary on the spot. I requested that he send all correspondence to my parents' Saratoga address. His letters were then digitized by my parents and emailed to me. Although it wasn't the most effective system, it did the job. We were able to exchange almost a dozen letters by the time I got to Livingston.

Now that our visit is just a daybreak away, I stretch out on the bed and start reading through the pile of letters. Sincere, humorous, and fast to reply, Lil' GQ has been a great pen friend. Over the years, he had developed correspondences with dozens of people, so he had a lot of experience. He claimed that when the jail guards arrived on "mail call" every night, it gave him something to do and something to anticipate. I like to write letters and pick up new skills from people who have accomplished far more than I have. You see, I dropped out of high school and have been incarcerated since I was 20. He acknowledged that the epistolary form also had a utilitarian function: since I stutter, writing letters enables me to express myself without feeling insecure or angry when I'm struggling to convey what I want to say.

I received letters from Lil' GQ about a variety of topics. He shared his interests with me in a letter: The best companion of a prisoner in solitary confinement is a book. He told me about his first vehicle, a brown Cadillac that had been stolen: I used to get up early, sit on my car's hood, and watch the projects come to life. He sent me a homemade card that read, "Courage! Survivor! Friendship!" and had a pink ribbon drawn on it in honor of Breast Cancer Awareness Month. Hero! Power! Generally speaking, Lil' GQ's tone was upbeat, but occasionally I got the impression that he was writing from a position of defeat: "Life around here has been the same ole routine for a brotha." He acknowledged that there were days when he had to find the will to continue, but he was always careful to avoid self-pity: I know that there are many others who would love to have as much free time as I do, but in a different situation.

At thirty-six, Lil' GQ had been on death row for nearly half of his life. He insisted that I tell him everything about the globe since he understood that a lot had changed "out there." I tried to keep him informed about my travels. From a Motel 6 in rural Iowa, I wrote to him. In Jackson, Wyoming, I wrote to him beside the fireplace of a mid-century modern mansion. After addressing an eighth-grade class at a Chicago public school, I wrote to him. When I showed Lil' GQ the poems the students had written in response to the topic, "where I'm from," he attempted to write his own: "I'm from where you didn't always feel a lot of love in the household." There are only gang members, drug dealers, and addicts everywhere where I come from. You're usually told that a hardhead is a soft behind where I'm from.

Lil' GQ added me to his visitation list as I approached Texas and explained the guidelines: The hours of operation for visitors would be 8:00 a.m. to 3:00 p.m. We would have to sit on different sides of a plexiglass divider and communicate with each other via telephone receivers because it would be a noncontact visit. He said, "Your time and presence is good enough for me," in response to my request to bring Lil' GQ books or anything else he might need. I can consider it a pre-Christmas gift.

My reading is interrupted by hollering and hooting outside the window. I place the pile of letters on the bed and get to my feet. I pull back the drapes and see the men from before. They moved to my car from the parking lot's nooks and crannies, and two of them sit on the back bumper as the others remain huddled in a half circle. I watch as the group's ringleader—the same guy who chased me—roars intoxicatedly as he dumps the leftovers of a forty-ounce beer over his head and slams the bottle onto the sidewalk. I take up the room phone and call reception, explaining the issue, feeling uneasy. A security guard walks over a few minutes later. Within minutes, everyone disperses, but I can't hear what he says.

I shut off the lights, pull the drapes closed, and go beneath the covers. Having yet another cold makes it difficult for me to sleep while I'm having trouble breathing, so I get up and go through my duffel bag in an attempt to find a bottle of leftover NyQuil. My thoughts quickly go sluggish as I pull the comforter over my head after taking a few swigs. I have no idea how long I've been asleep, but a monotonous, repetitive sound that keeps coming up in my dreams wakes me up in the middle of the night. With a moan, I turn over on my stomach and cover my head with a pillow. There is a brief pause in sound. Then, like a flurry, I hear it again: Bam. Bam. Bam. Oscar jumps off the bed, growling and barking, and I sit up startled. I fumble clumsily after him in the dark as I can't see anything without my contact lenses. It sounds like it's coming from behind the door of my motel room.

On the opposite side, a man says, "Open up." "Fucking open the door." Something about the slurred speech and the voice reminds me of the man from the parking lot, and I shudder when I identify it. I try to stifle Oscar's growls by squeezing him into my arms.

"Open the door. If you fail to open the damn door. I feel like I'm in grave danger for the first time since I've been driving. I am all too aware that all it takes is one unpleasant night or one person with bad news to make us rethink all that has happened before and after. The man's voice gets louder and more irate as he smacks his fist on the door until it rattles. With my entire body trembling and my brain desperately trying to make sense of what is occurring, I cower behind the door. I must be the one who alerted hotel security about the man and his companions. Perhaps I caused difficulties for them. He is furious because of this. I can't recall if I took it in from the car, but my mind goes to the little red can of pepper spray I have stashed away somewhere. Although I can't seem to move my limbs, let alone think clearly, I want to think that if this man succeeds to get in, I will be able to beat him off if necessary.

"Open the door, Pablo. Only when the man yells, "OPEN THE MOTHERFUCKING DOOR, PABLO!" do I finally get it. This man hasn't come for me; instead, he's searching for one of his pals, a man named Pablo, and in his drunken haze, he's ended up at my door by mistake. He gives up with a last, enraged slam of his fist. He stumbles down the corridor, and I watch through the peephole. For a long time, I stand there. I hold Oscar close to my chest and reassure myself that everything is fine. I'm all right. I'm secure. Now he's gone. I can't seem to stop shaking, though, no matter how many times I reassure myself.

For almost three months, I have been traveling alone, staying at the houses of people I know online, sleeping in truck stop parking lots and campgrounds, and sharing accommodations with random people I have met along the way. The world has welcomed me and shown me nothing but kindness at every turn. It wouldn't be an exaggeration to say that the road journey has restored my faith in people and given me a sense of power and independence that I had feared I would never regain. I have never felt more bold, more open to the unknown, or more clear-headed in my life than I have in the past few weeks. However, I've also been lucky, I realize tonight. As I go back to sleep, I can't quit thinking about it.

Texas's death row convicts are held in the infamous, all-male Allan B. Polunsky Unit. Situated in the densely forested Piney Woods, five miles outside of Livingston, it's not the kind of spot you find by chance. Under a flat, gray sky, I follow my GPS through countryside, turning left off the highway and past a mobile home park, a few churches, fields of horses, and abandoned cars.

A regiment of squat concrete buildings with hundreds of small slit windows can be seen behind the concertina-wire-topped chain-link fence that greets me as I approach the prison's gate. Lil' GQ is in his cell somewhere, behind one of these windows, getting ready for our visit. When I pull up to a guard's hut, a man in a uniform circles my car and taps the window, signaling for me to lower it. He asks, "Inmate ID number?"

My first of many mistakes that day was not writing down or memorizing Lil' GQ's ID number. The guard offers to check it out himself and assures me not to worry. "You travel from New York to come here?" he asks, looking at my driver's license.

I give a nod.

"That's dedication!" he exclaims. "You must be going to see someone very special."

I respond, "You could say that."

"I once visited New York City. In the 1970s, I served in the military in Germany and went through the airport. It wasn't really appealing to me. I'm a country boy. Are you originally from the Big Apple?"

"Yes, of course," I reply, nodding.

"You seem like a much nicer young woman than someone who lives in New York. There it is, then. A pleasant Texan and a pleasant New Yorker. Who would have guessed?

In addition to wishing me a Merry Christmas, the guard gives me a parking space in the adjacent lot. Our conversation gives me hope, but once I'm in the prison, I can't seem to do anything correctly. A woman in a uniform with bright red hair in a topknot stops me as soon as I enter the main building. She points at my pen, notebook, driver's ID, and car keys and says, "You can't bring all that stuff in here." "Everything must be placed in a transparent baggie. Have you got one?

I give a headshake. We march back out to the parking lot after she signals for me to follow her. She opens her car's trunk and takes out a large box of transparent plastic bags. "The Texas Department of Criminal Justice is responsible for keeping Ziploc operating."

After completing a few forms inside the prison, I am buzzed through a series of barred doors to the visiting room. A third guard greets me as I enter, takes my visitor's pass, and examines me from head to toe while narrowing her eyes at my Ziploc bag. Her tone is a little accusing as she says, "What do you have there?" "You should not have a pen or paper with you."

I stutter, "No one told me that."

She firmly declares, "If it happens again, you'll be banned from visiting," and takes them away. "Sit down in R28. Soon, the prisoner will be released.

I walk into a room filled with dozens of white cubicles that resemble phone booths, feeling shaken by our conversation. A plastic tree with ornaments by the door and a little play area with a rocking horse and a few toys seem out of place and somehow make the scene even more depressing. I walk over to R28 and sit down. As Lil' GQ mentioned in his letter, there is plexiglass in front of me and a phone receiver on my left. A cage-like booth and a stool that I assume he will sit on are located on the other side of the plexiglass. There isn't much privacy in the cubicles, and while I wait, I hear conversations going on. Three small children are seated to my left, speaking timidly to their father. A graying couple and their son are reciting their favorite Christmas carols to my right. Through a receiver, they croon softly, "Feliz Navidad, prospero año y felicidad."

After over 45 minutes of waiting, a door on the other side of the plexiglass wall clanks open. Little GQ enters. As a security removes his wrist and ankle cuffs, he smiles nervously at me. He's taller than I thought he would be, approximately five feet seven inches, beautiful, and sporting a new number two fade. He is wearing a white, short-sleeved jail jumpsuit that reveals tattooed, muscular arms. Lil' GQ sits down and grabs the receiver as a guard locks the door behind him. "I'm really n-n-nervous right now, so I apologize in advance if that keeps happening," he says. "I s-s-stutter when I get nervous."

I confess, "I'm also pretty nervous," which appears to calm him down. What does Lil' GQ stand for, anyway? That's what I've been meaning to ask you.

"Every Black person has a nickname, and mine is an abbreviation for Gangsta Quin. Have you got one?

"Susu. Growing up, they called me that since no one could pronounce my given name correctly.

He looks directly into my eyes and says, "Susu." "I enjoy that. Well, Susu, I wanted to thank you for coming here before we really get started with this visit. About ten years have passed since anyone paid me a visit, and I've been eagerly awaiting that day. For real.

Lil' GQ starts telling me everything about his life over the course of the following several hours, stories and recollections spilling out of his mouth as if I were a confessor and this was the last time he would ever share his story. He tells me about his five siblings, four of whom had also been imprisoned at different times. "There wasn't a lot of love shared between us," he tells me of his mother, who was the first to pull a gun on him. He tells me about his time living in a public housing project and about "Agg Land," a Southside community in Fort Worth that he represented. He tells me, his eyes sad, about the relative who began to abuse him in elementary school and how no one took him seriously when he told them about it. "I realized then that I would have to learn how to defend myself if I wanted to live in this world," he says.

Lil' GQ reveals a horrific scar, a welt of puckered skin in the shape of the letter C, pressing his forearm against the plexiglass. "C" stands for Crip, the infamous street gang, he explains. "Gang members command the most respect in the hood," he says me, describing how he knew that was what he wanted to be when he grew up, even in kindergarten. He tells me how, as a sign of loyalty, he branded his own skin at the age of twelve by heating the wire hook of a hanger over a cooktop flame. When he put a bullet through his palm on a dare, to the applause of other gang members, he showed me another scar—this one on his hand. He claims that despite his advanced age and frail physique, he wanted to demonstrate that he was a badass.

"What defines a badass as such?" I inquire.

"Violence" is the only word he uses in response.

When the guards aren't looking, Lil' GQ shows me a story map of his chest's burn marks, tattoos, and scars by unbuttoning the front of his jumpsuit. He informs me of another bullet wound he inflicted on his own body, this time on his rib cage. However, there are no applauding onlookers in this story. By the time he was fifteen, he had changed from the admired gangster he had envisioned to what he called "the lowest of life-forms inhabiting the hood"—a heroin dealer who had become an addict, draining the supply. He pulled out his gun one day while strolling down the street by himself, aimed it at his own chest, and squeezed the trigger. While his wound was being sutured, he awoke in the emergency department.

"What made you do it?" I inquire.

It perplexes you when someone you trust mistreats you. You begin to despise yourself when you remain perplexed. For a minute, a cloud covers his face and he becomes silent.

Asking him what brought him here seems like a decent idea at this point. Lil' GQ tells me straight out that he has committed other murders in addition to the one for which he is on death row. "Those other killings were gang-related, so I don't feel bad about them," he claims. The law of the jungle when you're from where I am is that if you don't shoot, they will. That's simply the reality. That last murder, the one for which I was prosecuted, was problematic since it involved a loved one. I needed more, and I was high on narcotics. However, I don't attribute my actions to the medications. For a long time, I thought I should have been executed because I was at blame.

How much of what Lil' GQ is telling me is accurate is unknown to me. I'm just listening; I'm not looking for contradictions, repetitions, gaps, or inconsistencies. I came here for other reasons, and this man has already been condemned for his actions. I nod, and sometimes I add a question or a "I hear that," but I listen most of the time. Even while I can't claim to understand much about his situation, I do relate to Lil' GQ's need to tell all of these experiences and his attempts to make sense of what has happened to him—even while he's on death row. There is a sense of urgency to take ownership of your life and create your legacy in your own words and on your own terms when you are forced to face your mortality, whether it is due to a diagnosis or a state-mandated death sentence. Telling stories about your life is a way to resist being boiled down to a simple matter of inevitable fate. This quote from Joan Didion, "We tell ourselves stories in order to live," comes to mind as I sit here listening to Lil' GQ talk. With the exception of Lil' GQ, who is narrating stories to himself to help him cope with death.

"What is the remaining number of appeals you have?" I inquire.

"Another one," he says. As he describes the steps leading up to execution, a vein in his forehead pulses. The legal notice informing you that a date has been set is delivered to your cell. Due to the high number of suicide attempts, the special section is where prisoners are moved sixty days before to execution and are monitored around-the-clock. "I don't ask my family to be present when I'm executed, but some individuals do. Instead of being laid down like a dog and strapped to a table, this is how I want to be remembered. No one should have that mental image. I'm going to leave this planet alone, just as I entered it alone.

I'm ready when I get back the following morning. I have twenty dollars in cash for the vending machines in case I need a snack, a clear plastic baggie for my wallet, and Lil' GQ's inmate ID number jotted down on a Post-it note. I make my way through the maze of corridors and checkpoints, and I'm relieved that no guards yell at me. Before Lil' GQ shows up on the other side of the oily plexiglass partition, everything looks to be going according to plan. I see huge bags under his eyes that weren't there yesterday, and he appears distressed.

"How are you feeling?" I inquire.

To be honest? He fidgets with the receiver wire and informs me, "I didn't sleep." "I started talking like a fool yesterday, trying to impress you and all that because I was so scared. I was certain that I had insulted you or that you believed me to be a psychotic murderer when you departed," he says. In the cell next door, I informed my homie that I was certain you wouldn't return. In order to properly convey myself in the event that you did, I spent the entire night organizing and writing down my ideas.

Lil' GQ stoops and digs into his sneaker. He produces a piece of paper that has been folded into a small square. I notice that there are notes all over it as he opens it. He starts reading from a list of inquiries. He inquires about my family and health. He wants to read my favorite book, so he asks what it is. He wants to know what kind of music I like and what breed Oscar is. He wants to know what I did while I was in the hospital. I tell him, "I got really, really good at Scrabble."

"Really? I agree! Even though I'm not very skilled at Scrabble, I'm giving it a shot. When he describes how he and his other inmates make their own board games out of paper and shout their moves through the vents in the cells where they get their lunch trays, his entire face beams. He informs me that they can play a variety of games in this manner, including cards and backgammon.

Although Lil' GQ claims he has never been ill in his life and begins his day with a thousand push-ups, he can relate to a lot of my experience with cancer. He knows the loneliness and claustrophobia of being confined to a small room for extended periods of time, the feeling of being imprisoned in purgatory while waiting for the word of your fate, and how you have to be creative to stay sane. It was these surprising similarities that first inspired him to write to me. Lil' GQ states, "You've faced death in your own personal prison just as I continue to face death in mine." "Death is death at the end of the day, regardless of the form it takes."

The similarities between our experiences are limited, despite our best efforts to reach through the plexiglass and meet in a shared space that we both comprehend. Striking a balance between finding meaning in someone else's narrative and minimizing your own sorrow is difficult. In addition to the apparent disparities in privilege, gender, and education, as well as skin color, the fact that I am traveling to see Lil' GQ highlights a fundamental difference: His is a body in prison; mine is a body in motion. For the remainder of our visit, however, we act as though we are in a coffee shop, merely two individuals conversing and making an effort to relate to one another, albeit clumsily.

I jump when someone taps my shoulder. A guard has arrived to inform us that it is 3:00 p.m. Lil GQ declares, "My time is up." He asks me one last question before I go. "Would you take everything back if you could?"

If I could undo everything? I am in disbelief. "I'm not sure," I mutter.

These are the final miles I have left. As I drive through Louisiana's bayous, insects splash across the windshield. On the Alabama coast, I get trapped in a storm, have engine problems since I forgot to change my oil, and stay at the aptly called Comfort Inn close to Daytona Beach, where I wake up to find that I have fleas all over me. A beautiful night of camping on Georgia's Jekyll Island, with the sound of the waves lulling me to sleep, is how I start the new year. In Charleston, I stay with an old crush and receive my first speeding ticket, which my mother says should be my last. I pause briefly before slithering back up the East Coast to cross off one last name on my list: Unique, a tiny adolescent girl who has lived in hospital rooms for the majority of her adolescence but is now getting ready to join the larger group. I ask her what she wants to do next over lunch. From the other side of the table, she smiles at me with a brightness that makes me feel as though I'm in the sun: "I want to go to college! And go! And consume strange meals that I've never tried, like octopus! And come to New York to see you! And go camping! I want to go camping even if I'm afraid of bugs! Perhaps it's her positivity, the lengthy journey, or the awareness that my time on the road is almost over, but as I bite into a salty fry, I think to myself, "This is the most delicious fry I've ever tasted."

I keep thinking about Lil' GQ's question as I continue to drive. I see Will showing up at my door in Paris, both of us so naive and full of promise. I recall my father's bloodshot eyes every time he came home from his walks in the woods, and my mother's battered face when the doctor gave me my diagnosis. I recall my brother's poor academic performance in his senior year, the stress he endured as my donor, and how my needs were always prioritized before his. I hear echoes in the silence before bed: the animal cries of sorrow, those soft groans of pain. Naturally, I would stop at nothing to protect my loved ones from suffering, fear, and heartbreak. Of course, if I hadn't gotten sick, it would have been simpler.

Then I think of all the things I wrote while in bed, the letters I got, and the unexpected connections I formed. I reach back to pat Oscar, who is dozing off in the backseat, at a stoplight. If it weren't for the isolation of hospital rooms and the cancerous cells that bound us together, I would never have met Max, Melissa, and everyone else. I go back and review the roads, campgrounds, and reckonings I've made over the past three months. I see everyone who has challenged me to reach new heights: Ned, Cecelia, Howard, Nitasha, Bret, Salsa, Katherine, and everyone else. As I pitched my tent for the first time, I heard the wind howling over the Pine Ridge plains, the squawking of a fat russet hen being chased around and around a barn, the high-up branches of the redwoods cracking in the cool ocean air, and the satisfying crunch of pinecones beneath my boots.

My twenties have been the most formative years of my life, filled with the sweet grace of a second chance and an abundance of luck, if such a concept can be said to exist at all, despite the fact that they have also been wrenching, confusing, and difficult—to the point where they have occasionally felt unbearably painful. My life has become a bizarre, discordant scene due to the tangle of so much beauty and violence. Though it has given me a jeweler's eye, it has also left me with an awareness that lingers on the periphery of my vision—it might all be gone in an instant.

I would not change my diagnosis if I could, if I were thinking about my condition without considering how it affects those around me. I wouldn't take back the pain I went through to obtain this.

Copyright © 2025

All rights reserved

The content of this book may not be reproduced, duplicated, or transmitted without the author's or publisher's express written permission. Under no circumstances will the publisher or author be held liable or legally responsible for any damages, reparation, or monetary loss caused by the information contained in this book, whether directly or indirectly.

Legal Notice:
This publication is copyrighted. It is strictly for personal use only. You may not change, distribute, sell, use, quote, or paraphrase any part of this book without the author's or publisher's permission.

Disclaimer Notice:
Please keep in mind that the information in this document is only for educational and entertainment purposes. Every effort has been made to present accurate, up-to-date, reliable, and comprehensive information. There are no express or implied warranties. Readers understand that the author is not providing legal, financial, medical, or professional advice. This book's content was compiled from a variety of sources. Please seek the advice of a licensed professional before attempting any of the techniques described in this book. By reading this document, the reader agrees that the author is not liable for any direct or indirect losses incurred as a result of using the information contained within this document, including, but not limited to, errors, omissions, or inaccuracies.

Printed in Dunstable, United Kingdom